# Marketing FOR Million$

Secrets of Top Producing
Financial Planners

by *James Hug*

# Table Of Contents

## Target Markets

## Turning Targets Into Prospects

## Seminar Marketing

## Turning Prospects Into Clients

# Introduction

"If it was easy, everyone would do it."

 The person who coined that phrase was probably referring to marketing a financial practice. Just imagine how easy your life would be if you could simply send a letter or postcard to your best prospects, and a few days later have your phone start ringing and your door start swinging. Many have tried it – most have failed.

The days of do-it-yourself marketing are over. Your ideal prospects are way too savvy. They have to be – everybody wants their dollar. Not only are your prospects getting wiser, so are your competitors. More advisors are marketing their practices than ever before. CPAs, banks – even grocery stores – are offering advisory services. If it seems like everyone is after your best prospects, you're right.

To successfully compete in today's market, you need to stand out from the crowd. You need a professional look, a compelling message, and a proven concept. Otherwise, you will be throwing your money away.

In this book, we share our knowledge gained from hands-on financial marketing experience. We have invested countless hours and hundreds of thousands of dollars creating and implementing a multitude of marketing programs; testing and retesting these programs to the point of perfection -- or as close as it's going to get.

These efforts have not only resulted in the products we offer, but an entire marketing philosophy (which you will see unfold over the course of this book). In essence, we're providing you with a road map to financial marketing success. We have already taken all the wrong turns and found all the pot holes and dead ends. We'll show you what works, and more importantly, *why*.

All of the marketing strategies and techniques in this book are currently being used by top producing financial advisors. We know they work, because we see the results our clients get every single day.

Read the book with an open mind. Some of it may not apply directly to you and your market, but there is something in here for every advisor. The important point to remember is that every approach and tactic detailed in <u>Marketing for Millions</u> has worked for other advisors just like you.

If you stick with what's known to work and has been tested by others you are much more likely to achieve great results. Many advisors swear by seminars; others prefer direct mail campaigns. But the most successful top producers develop a comprehensive marketing mix that also includes drip marketing, personal branding, educational marketing, and more. The key is to find the mix that works for *you*.

Once you have a system in place, it's just a matter of repeating it again and again to steadily build your practice to a level you never thought possible. It won't happen overnight, but it will happen. Find what works for you and stick to it. Before you know it, you will be *Marketing for Millions*.

If you have questions, or would like information on any of the proven products we offer here at Acquire Direct Marketing, we are always happy to help. Give us a call at 800-771-9898 or drop an e-mail to info@acquiredm.com.

Sincerely,

James Hug,
President
Acquire Direct Marketing
www.acquirefinancial.com

# Are You A Visionary?

Visionaries are always well informed. Although the word "visionary" implies some sort of dreamlike approach, the opposite is true. They are pragmatic. Once the initial excitement over a new idea has passed, they don't proceed without doing their research and making sure their new idea is grounded in reality.

Basically, visionaries are problem solvers; they often do so by breaking the accepted rules. They are also quite willing to break from tradition. Visionaries are able to see what is not working. Most visionary financial advisors are truly self-made men who don't come with a string of degrees, but have learned by trial and error what works for their specific personality, in their specific marketplace.

Visionaries often start small but know when and how to get other people on board. They have an innate sense of timing. They also know whom to bring on board. If they cannot afford to hire staff full-time, they are not afraid of outsourcing.

Visionaries look for the right signs. They will often test markets rather than rely on what they *think* is true. They know that what is most important about a service or a product is whether or not people are willing to buy it. After all, people vote with their dollars.

Visionaries don't get bogged down. They are willing to fight up-hill -- but only for a finite amount of time. Then, they either move on or decide they don't have to convince everybody their idea is perfect; they just have to locate like-minded people to sell.

Most importantly, visionaries don't buy into the myths. The greatest myth about marketing that financial advisors often buy into, is that it is merely a numbers game. A visionary knows how simplistic this concept is. Successful marketing requires focus, expertise and economy - not gross numbers. Any marketing campaign will probably have to be tweaked more than once to yield maximum results. The key is knowing how and what changes to make.

Don't underestimate what a complex task the marketing of financial services and products really is. The reason is simple but crucial: you are dealing with the most emotionally loaded issue that most people confront -- their own money. After all, money means security, or, in other words, self-preservation.

Are you ready?

# What Is Marketing?

The practice of marketing is almost as old as humanity itself. Whenever a person has an item or is capable of performing a service, he or she seeks another person who might want that item or that service. This is marketing in a nutshell.

The practice has evolved over the years and become the subject of a great deal of study. Some people claim marketing is an art, while others insist it is a science. At the extreme, two recognized experts in the field of marketing, Al Ries and Jack Trout, define it simply as "war between competitors".

But fighting about the definition obscures one of the primary benefits of marketing itself. At its best, it is a process that raises our standard of living by first identifying the existing problems and unsatisfied needs of people. Only then can one solve the problem or satisfy the need with a product or service that delivers value to the customer. Clearly this is a definition of marketing that views it as a benign or even helpful force.

Prior to the beginning of market research, most companies were product focused. They employed teams of salespeople to push their products on the market regardless of the market's desires. But the advent of market research brought about the beginnings of customer-focused organizations. These companies completely changed the methodology of marketing by first determining what a potential customer desires, and then creating a product or service to meet that need.

Financial advisory practices should be the ultimate customer focused organizations. Discovering customer needs and satisfying them is the only way to build a business – especially one that depends so much on the retention of clients and client referrals.

Retention of clients is known as "base management" and it is considered an integral part of marketing. The process of base management shifts the marketing process to the challenge of building relationships by nurturing the links between the advisor and the client. It's all about enhancing the benefits that sold the client in the first place. Meanwhile, the advisor should be continuously improving the product or service he offers in the ongoing effort to protect his business from his competitors. Good marketers require knowledge of economics, psychology, sociology, and strategy to create an advantage over other practices.

Marketing has been divided by the academics into three levels: corporate, business, and functional. For the individual financial advisor, the corporate level is something he or she has no control over. However, for the independent advisor, the business level is important because it addresses strategic concerns. The most critical of these is how you create sustainable advantages over your competitors and how you create a business model to deliver them.

Marketing at the functional level asks the most basic question, "How do you create and keep customers?" A marketing mix known as "the four Ps" has been identified as a way to systematically answer this critical question. The four Ps are:

1.  **Product** – This deals with the specifications of the actual goods and services to be sold and how that relates to the consumers' needs and wants.

2.  **Pricing** – This usually refers to not only setting a price, but also providing discounts. In the world of the financial

advisor, the pricing focus is all about the method of charging the client for services and products. The choice, depending on one's circumstances, is whether to be fee based, transaction based, or a combination of both.

3. **Promotion** – This includes advertising, publicity, the selling process, and the methods of promoting your service or product

4. **Placement** – This refers to how a product or service is delivered to your customer. The average financial advisor is working at the retail sales level in person, generally under written agreement.

While these "four Ps" are referred to by scholars as the "marketing mix", they can be used in real life to help create a marketing plan. In addition there are four other Ps to consider. They are:

1. **People** – This refers not just to the financial advisor, but also to his employees who are an important part of his total service. Everyone involved must be well trained and highly motivated. An emerging area of study and practice concerns internal marketing, or how your employees are trained and managed to deliver your brand in the optimal way.

2. **Process** – This is the manner in which one sells a product or service. This is considered one of the most crucial elements in client satisfaction.

3. **Physical Evidence** – Unlike a product, a service is an intangible which can't be experienced before it is delivered. The financial advisor is usually limited to using case stud-

ies, referrals, and testimonials to provide the "evidence" needed for marketing.

4. **Philosophy** – This is the last of the secondary Ps. All products and services should be in harmony with the underlying ethics of your practice.

These are the textbook definitions and components of marketing. The true challenge lies in taking and using them to gain a competitive advantage in the real world of financial services.

# Why Market Your Financial Planning Practice?

**M**arketing is all about persuasion. As a financial advisor, persuasion plays a vital role in your profession as well. In fact, before reading this book, you must answer this question truthfully, "In your heart of hearts are you a financial advisor, or are you an entrepreneur who happens to be in the business of delivering financial advice?"

Probably, you are a bit of both. But if you describe yourself *primarily* as a financial advisor, you are most likely content with the status quo, or growing your business about 10% per year. In the back of your mind you may worry about becoming overextended and working many more hours than you already do. After all, it will be pretty hard to deliver the great service that you extol if you build your practice above 150 clients or so. That would mean taking on another professional with extra support staff, and now you are going to have to become a manager! Better to let things stay as they are for a while, and let your business grow without actively marketing. Better just to remain comfortable and depend on referrals.

However, if you are a true entrepreneur, you can't stand to stay still. To you, "marketing" and "selling" are not dirty words. They stand for a challenging and enjoyable process that can be honed and perfected to build a practice with as much transferable value as possible. You know the most crucial step to success is marketing.

Unfortunately, because results from marketing campaigns have traditionally been difficult to quantify, funds for marketing are usually one of the first budget items to be cut. Marketing often gets relegated to a wish list, rather than remaining imperative to the success of your practice.

But consider this, the average financial advisor sees only two to four new prospects a month! You could be seeing at least four new prospects a *day*. This book is designed to give you the tools to help you get there. Putting your money into a well-constructed, ongoing marketing campaign can lead to big financial rewards. Of course there are many variables that influence your income, but the ideas you will find in the following pages are the same ones that have yielded other advisors incomes of **more than $1,000,000 a year**.

There is no doubt that these are the best of times to be a financial advisor. There are more products and strategies available than ever before to help your clients plan and save for retirement. The members of the baby boom era are just beginning to hit retirement age; bringing with them a staggering amount of wealth. This is the first generation where much of that wealth will be in self-directed instruments such as IRAs and 401(k)s, creating endless opportunities for financial advisors. Not only will the boomers bring their own accumulated wealth, they will also be inheriting money at unprecedented levels.

With such lofty projections for the financial services industry as a whole, you may be wondering why you even need to market. The reason is simple: *competition*.

Although the pool of prospective clients gets larger every day, so does the number of advisors who want to manage and reposition their money. To succeed in this competitive climate, you need to make yourself and your practice stand out from the crowd. To do that, you need to market. Even advisors, who in the past have enjoyed slow but steady growth solely through referrals, will most likely have to do some form of marketing to maintain that level of growth in the face of increased competition.

And, that competition is not just coming from other "traditional" financial planners. There are many other professions and corporations who now want a piece of the financial planning pie.

For years there have been CPAs who also provide services as financial advisors. But now there are national organizations which specialize in training CPAs to create a dual practice. For them it is a perfect fit because many CPAs already have a large base of clients who regard them as their most trusted advisor. And they already have access to their clients' tax returns, which they can use as a road map to better their clients' financial position. The irony of this is that many regular financial advisory firms are hiring a tax specialist at least part time and rebranding themselves as tax advisory services in order to take advantage of the most trusted advisor role enjoyed by CPAs.

On the national level, competition is now coming at you from companies which have an established brand they want to leverage into the financial services industry. As a result, financial advisors are popping up in some pretty unexpected places these days.

The most extreme example of this started in a grocery store chain in Canada known as Loblaws. About 15 years ago they decided to produce their own house brand of chocolate chip cookie known as "President's Choice". Because of a reputation for quality that surpassed the competition, the number of food items sold under the name grew and grew. Eventually, President's Choice products made their way onto American grocery store shelves as well.

About three years ago, executives in Canada decided to take the highly respected brand in a whole new direction -- money management. Both inside and outside the grocery stores, banners appeared touting "President's Choice" financial services. Now you could discuss your money market fund inside a cubicle, designed to look like an upscale office, at the grocery store . They even dropped literature advertising President's Choice Financial Services into bags at the checkout counter.

Another major threat to traditional financial advisors comes from banks, which are expanding into new areas of the financial services arena. They are doing so with great zeal, underwritten by very deep pockets. They also have a measure of credibility and vast corporate reach.

There is a true story of a lady who went through the drive-in teller at her branch of Bank of America to deposit a $300,000 check from the sale of her home. She couldn't understand why a transaction that would normally take only two or three minutes was taking closer to ten. Finally, the reason became apparent. One of the vice-presidents of the branch ran out in front of her car and yelled, "Stop! Promise you won't do anything with this money until you have talked with one of our financial advisors first."

No doubt you have noticed the direct mail marketing campaigns for various financial services that come with your own monthly bank statements and credit card bills. Companies are able to piggyback this extra promotion for pennies per piece. At one point

American Express was even offering 500 frequent flyer miles to anyone who would simply *meet* with one of their financial advisors.

This scale of marketing is impossible for the independent advisor to match. Fortunately, financial advisors are in a relationship business. Huge corporations are trying to commoditize the industry, but they may have limited success. Although large institutions can make it easy for a client to invest a few thousand dollars in a CD, they have great difficulty in providing personalized service. The prospects you can appeal to the most are those who will value the long term personal service you can give them.

This is the reason you need to market constantly in a way that emphasizes the special individualized care you give each and every client. Unlike the big institutions, you can, and *should*, carve out an area of expertise and aim at targets of your own choosing. Nothing can replace the years of experience you have in building, protecting and distributing your clients' wealth with your own mix of products and services.

Remember, the only way that desirable prospects are going to find you amid the clutter of all the new competition is to send your message out loud and clear. To do that in the best manner possible, pay attention to the details.

This book is the result of many years of experience working with hundreds of financial advisors. It will show you not just how, but also why, to market your financial advisory practice in an increasingly competitive environment.

# Target
# Markets

# Choosing Your Targets

Before you initiate any kind of marketing, there is something critical that you must do; you must define your target market or markets. One of the most important lessons you can take away from this book is that *you can't fight your demographics*. You must have a large enough pool of prospects to draw clients from, or you will struggle forever just to keep your business going.

No matter how long you have maintained a business in your area, you still need to ensure you are dealing with the realities of your market. Most advisors feel the local clientele is wealthier than it truly is. Part of this is simply wishful thinking. You may have a few clients with a high net worth and assume that there are many more out there, if you could just get to them.

It is also easy to misinterpret visual cues suggesting affluence. Americans often believe in instant gratification. We are a "show off society". We drive more expensive cars than we should. We buy larger and fancier homes than we can truly afford. The fact is, behind the gates of many of those expensive homes, people are struggling just to pay their bills, and have little left over to sock away for a nest egg.

As you read this chapter, take an honest look at where you are currently focusing your marketing and referral efforts. Regardless of your situation or location, chances are you'll discover a few additional prospecting sources you can tap into without a great deal of additional work.

## Targeting Geographically

There are several ways to define your geographic market. Many advisors draw a 10 mile radius around their office and assume that is their target area. Others figure most prospects won't drive more than 20 minutes for an appointment. That may have been true in the past, but with today's encroaching traffic gridlock, people have become used to spending more time behind the wheel every time they pull out of their garage. Different areas of the country -- and the people who live there -- are so diverse, it's impossible to come up with a rule of thumb that is applicable to every market.

For example, prospects in Houston think nothing of driving for an hour to an important appointment. (And, of course, meeting with you is definitely to be considered an important appointment.) By contrast, the residents of Tampa and St. Petersburg, Florida won't make the 10 minute drive across the bridge that separates the two cities; except for attending football games or flying out of the airport. You probably have an innate sense of just how far prospects are willing to drive to see you. The only way to know for sure is to test your marketing in the areas on the outskirts of what you consider to be your main target area; and monitor the results. You may be surprised to find that your area is larger than you thought.

The other thing you should do is go through your list of clients and categorize which zip codes they reside in. Then, you need to ask yourself whether the geographic distribution of your clients is an accurate reflection of your market, or if maybe these are the only zip codes where you have made an effort to market. Again, your market may be broader than you think it is.

You can get a true demographic breakdown of your area from a national list compiler or financial seminar marketing company.

(Chapter 13 deals with lists in much greater detail.) No matter who you contact, you should make it clear that you are not yet ready to buy a list of names. All you are looking for at this point is a count. Give them a list of zip codes that are within your targeted driving area, and ask for a breakdown by age and income.

Ideally you are looking for a group of prospects in your area that comprises a list of 15,000 - 30,000 names. This allows you to do a direct mail piece or seminar mailing to 5,000 - 10,000 households per month without repeating until the next quarter. (There are some drip mail programs which are best repeated monthly, but those are for special circumstances.)

Using the marketing model of 10,000 names per month, suppose you receive a rate of 1% and you convert only 10% of those to clients. This should bring you 30 new clients per quarter. That adds up to a low-ball estimate of 120 new clients per year. While this may not sound like an overwhelming number, it is far more than most independent advisors are able to acquire. And remember, these are the results from just one type of marketing campaign. You should never restrict yourself to just one marketing method.

## Not Everyone Wants To Work With The Wealthy

So far we have been looking at targeting, only from the perspective of hard numbers, but your own preferences are important too. If you don't like the type of clients you are working with, you will be miserable, and ultimately your emotions are bound to affect your bottom line. The question is, "What kinds of people do you most enjoy helping?"

There are many advisors who could go after wealthier clients, but say they don't find the work as psychologically rewarding. You often hear about culling your list of clients and dropping the "C" clients to go after more "A's." It goes without saying that "A" means your wealthiest clients. However, there are a surprising number of advisors out there who have thought a lot about what kinds of people they are most comfortable with and relate to best. Instead of targeting the so-called "A" prospects, they prefer the "B's" or "C's".

Since the majority of advisors who do major marketing campaigns tend to focus on households with assets of $300,000 and up, this leaves a good majority of the population as a relatively untouched target. Most advisors find that no matter what group they prefer, they usually still have at least a few clients in each category. The only caution here is that you will have to service a fairly large number of clients and have products that will yield enough income to make a practice, based on lower net worth candidates, sustainable. Fortunately, due to advances in technology and outsourcing, maintaining a large client base has become far more feasible. You may find yourself feeling well rewarded in terms of client gratitude and loyalty. And, there is the undeniable satisfaction of taking someone from a state of financial dependence to financial freedom.

In general, marketing campaigns seem to break down into three groups. The first group includes those with assets of $500,000 and below. The second group has assets from $500,000 to $1 million. The third includes those above the $1 million mark. Needless to say, the marketing approach to each group should be vastly different.

## *Secondary Targets*

We have talked about going after the group in your area that is the largest in sheer numbers while keeping in mind your comfort level. But we have not talked about secondary targets. No doubt your competitors have also run the numbers and are concentrating on the same major target you are: retirees with a specific level of investable assets. But remember, it is dangerous to focus only on one kind of marketing and only on one target.

In selecting your secondary targets, you should be focusing on any unmet needs that you discover. Ask your friends and neighbors to save all the mailings they get from competing financial firms over a three-month period. In the meantime, clip out relevant ads from your local newspaper, weekly community newspapers and city magazines. Look for the gaps in services being offered (i.e. college funding or long term care). Filling those gaps can be a great basis for secondary marketing campaigns. These prospects can become your secondary targets.

Another decision you must make in choosing your target market is deciding whom you *don't* wish to work with. In other words, are there certain types of people you would rather avoid? A study conducted by Source, Inc. asked 200 advisors this question, and found the number one target to avoid are prospects in the engineering profession. The reason most often given is that engineers typically possess highly analytical minds which can make them skeptics, and therefore, very wary of accepting the advice and reasoning of a financial advisor. However, if we may rework a common phrase, one man's poison is another man's meat. For example, the Source, Inc. survey found one advisor in Las Vegas who happens to be a former physicist. He likes nothing better than working with engineers, because he finds they attack problems the same way he does. In essence, they speak the same language. As such, he has received a great number of referrals. He has built his practice on the very same engineers that his competitors don't want to deal with.

Another professional group that advisors find difficult to work with is physicians. Advisors often call them unapproachable and arrogant. But if this is true, think about the reasons for their behavior. They are constantly being approached by everyone from financial advisors to pharmaceutical salesmen. That cuts into the time they need to spend treating patients, as well as doing tedious government and insurance paperwork. Out of necessity, they have had to develop strong gatekeepers, or they would spend all their time listening to sales pitches.

The other problem physicians face is that they don't just work during the day; they are frequently on call for nighttime emergencies and must be up at the crack of dawn to make hospital rounds before they ever get to their office. This is the one group that is almost impossible to penetrate by any other means than referrals and drip marketing. The good news is that once you penetrate a medical practice, your name is often passed along to others in the same medical building or within the same specialty.

Many advisors say they don't like to work with the very elderly or, to be specific, people 80 and older. Usually these prospects think they have done all the financial and estate planning they are ever going to do. They can also be harder to reach because they are less likely to go out to events like dinner seminars. The prejudice against elderly prospects is particularly unfortunate, because this group constitutes the fastest-growing market in America and there are many new products that are particularly appropriate for them. A good approach to reach this target is to market to their adult children, (there are mailing lists available that reach this market).

In contrast, many financial advisors avoid the relatively young. In this case "young" means anyone under 50. These people often have their cash flow eaten up by mortgages, car payments, raising children, paying for college, and sometimes, subsidizing their own elderly parents. This leaves little money left over for investments. However, financial professionals, with a great deal of patience, who are willing to work with their clients over a fairly long time frame by helping them budget, build their assets, and stay out of debt, will reap a reward. The reward will be a base of financially desirable clients who will have at least 20 to 30 good years of financial planning and investing with you.

This may sound like an odd analogy, but consider the concept of laddering bonds. There is something to be said for the concept of laddering clients by age increments -- if you can acquire younger clients without too much time and expense. When each group reaches the age when they begin to think about retirement, they "come due" and are ready to invest in your retirement strategies and products.

## *Targeting Across Ethnic Boundaries*

There is the question of whether or not you can market across ethnic boundaries. Some advisors feel so strongly that ethnicity is an insurmountable barrier, that they put filters on the last names on their mailing lists because they believe certain groups will never become their clients no matter what approach they use. This can also work in reverse. An advisor who is from a large, well-represented ethnic group may filter out names of all prospects that are not of the same origin. Basically they are targeting only their own nationality or language.

It is important to know if your target group is large enough to sustain a practice. You can request this information by using a filter as part of your zip code count conducted through your mailing list provider.

## *Targeting Businesses*

So far, we have talked about targets comprised of individual households. But there is another side to the coin, and that is marketing to businesses. There are two ways to do this. The first is to target business owners with a focus on such issues as succession planning and special retirement strategies. The other potential target is to concentrate on the needs of their employees. If the business is a large one, you may find yourself going through the director of human resources or another high-level employee, but you will still usually need the blessing of the owners or board of directors.

Often, advisors completely ignore targeting businesses because they are so unfamiliar in terms of approach and products. But doing so has one simple advantage; you can often target businesses much more affordably than households. Since the "do not call list" went into effect, it is virtually impossible to reach qualified individual households by telemarketing. Even if you do somehow manage to obtain a list of numbers you are permitted to call, you will find yourself calling the same small group of people over and over again; probably to the point where they stop taking your calls.

By contrast, you are free to contact business prospects by phone. Your local Yellow Pages directory is an excellent source for prospects. Most are arranged by business type or SIC, (Standard Industrial Classification), codes. Business mailing lists are available from your mailing list provider. To better qualify your prospects, you can select by SIC code, employee size, and even sales volume. Another advantage to targeting businesses is that you can go farther geographically than you can when targeting households. Since businesses expect you to come to them, driving time becomes much less of an issue.

While marketing to businesses can be profitable, dealing with businesses can involve far more complex issues, and requires longer timelines than marketing to households. When you are deciding on your primary target audience, you should choose one or the other, unless you are in an area with so few leads, you are forced to target both households and businesses.

## *Targeting Where There Are Few Prospects*

There is one targeting problem we have yet to touch. What if your office is in a rural area with such a small population you can't come up with a sufficient number of leads nearby? Quite simply, no matter how distant they may be, you are going to have to go to them. For example, there is a highly motivated advisor located deep within the coal country of Pennsylvania, who pulls in over $1 million a year. He gets in his car, gives seminars over a 100 mile radius, stays in motels, and services his clients by going to their homes. If he can make that kind of money with that kind of demographic, so can you.

While expanding your market is a necessity in rural areas, sometimes it is profitable in metro areas as well. Atlanta is a wealthy city where one would assume ideal targets are sitting right on everyone's doorstep. However, the competition there is so fierce that several advisors are broadening their marketing area in search of new prospects. Some are even on a circuit that takes them as far away as Valdosta, which is only 20 minutes from the Florida border -- a drive of more than 200 miles from the home office! These advisors have indeed learned that you can't fight demographics. Unfortunately, they have also decided that their only option is to literally go to great lengths to work with viable prospects.

Choosing your targets based upon the realities of your market area will put the rest of your marketing plan on much firmer ground.

# Targeting Retirees

The average age of retirement in America today is 57 according, to the Federal government. How can that possibly be? Don't most people retire when they reach age 65, or wait at least until the minimum age of 62?

Most likely, the numbers are skewed by the fact that the statistics refer to the population as a whole, and not just to the primary breadwinner. Women who work, cease to do so at much earlier ages than their male counterparts; they often retire when they begin to have children. When you look at it this way, 57 becomes a little more plausible.

The problem is that when most financial advisors market to retirees, they target those age 60 or 65 and up. If you assume this makes sense because most men are still part of the workforce until age 65, you are missing two very important points. First of all, you are underestimating the role women play in investment decisions. Secondly, you have no chance of capturing those wealthy enough to retire young. If your market is retirees, you should definitely include prospects as young as 55.

By changing your target demographic by as little as five years, you will become more inclusive. However, your marketing will also have to become more sophisticated and more complex because you will also be hitting the first wave of the Baby Boomers. There is a wide divergence in the attitudes and concerns of a 55 year old prospect and one who is 75.

Many marketing gurus, who give advice on marketing to retirees, still assume that all of today's male retirees were soldiers who fought in World War II. They are basing that advice on demographic profiles from 10 years ago. Even if you assume your prospects were the minimum age of 17 at the beginning of America's entry into the war, that would mean your lobby is populated with prospects who are all well into their 80's.

Frankly, it is highly unlikely that your next new client was once Rosie the Riveter. Quite simply, you may be advised to present yourself in a manner that misses the mark badly. It is time to end the condescension and the pandering. You can start by taking the word "senior" out of your vocabulary. You should also advise your staff that older female clients hate to be referred to as "sweetie" or "honey". They dislike being touched while being guided to your office. Save this kind of familiarity for your grandparents.

If your target is retirees, you have probably also been told that you should be practicing in a retirement haven like Florida or Arizona. Leave that to the advisors who are already established there. For example, Sarasota, Florida lists over 220 financial advisors in the phone book. And, that number doesn't include the wirehouses!

Demographic studies show that, nowadays, retirees usually stay closer to home, often moving 50 miles or less, although they may sometimes switch to a smaller abode.

But how on earth do you wrap your arms around a group as diverse as today's retirees? Author Ken Dychtwald attempted to do this in his book, Age Wave, published in 1990. Even though his paradigm is several years old, it still holds true today. Dychtwald believed that America would become a "gerontocracy", a society increasingly dominated by older people. He predicted that the emergence of this new class would bring about four outcomes:

1. More of us will live longer than any previous generation.
2. The epicenter of economic power will shift from the young to the old
3. We will need to change our current mindset about how we spend our extra years of life
4. How we decide to behave as elders will become the most important challenge we will face in our lives.

Dychtwald also coined the term "retirement happiness equation", which acknowledged that financial preparation for and during retirement plays a significant role in determining what type of retiree we will become. Using this equation, he broke down today's retirees into four different groups:

1. 27% are the "Ageless Explorers". They personify the new ideal retirement. They would rather be too busy than risk being bored, which makes them the second easiest group to market to with methods like seminars. They are in control of their lives (which means, unfortunately, they may already have advisors) and they are pushing the envelope while chasing new adventures. A solid 73% contributed to IRAs, and about half had 401(k)s. Roughly 65% invested in stock and mutual funds, and around half also invested in real estate and bonds.
2. 22% are called "Live for Todays". This group dreams of having time to do the things they didn't have time for earlier in life, and they are likely to say they never feel elderly inside. However, they are not as well prepared financially as they would like to be (this makes them great targets), but on the whole they are enjoying their new life. During their years of preparing for retirement, an average of 35 to 40% of them invested in various taxable and tax-advantaged accounts.

3.  19% are "Comfortable Contents". They look at retirement like a good pair of shoes that fit just right. Their's is a traditional view of retirement. Their finances are solidly in place, and they just love relaxing while enjoying their golden years. Their pre-planning financial profile isn't all that different from the "Ageless Explorer". They seem more like people satisfied with enjoying a quiet retirement. Their relative complacency makes them less likely to be looking for a new advisor.

4.  At 32%, the "Sick and Tireds" make up the largest group; and as Baby Boomers age, their contingent is bound to grow much larger. This group is comprised of the less than fortunate retirees who failed to prepare sufficiently and aren't happy about retirement at all. Only about 20 to 25% contributed to IRAs and 401(k)s in their early years. Very few put much money away in taxable accounts. This is the group that needs your help the most. The question is, can you and your practice afford to help them?

Dychtwald's studies are helpful because they raise some intriguing questions about marketing to retirees. Notice the categories are arranged mostly as psychological profiles with no real numbers on investable assets or income attached. In order to be realistic about where you should spend your marketing dollars, you will need to establish income/asset criteria in order to figure out your cost/benefit ratio. This is particularly true of the last group. The key to marketing to this group is to let them know their limited assets should not intimidate them from seeking a financial advisor. You may possibly still be able to help them by putting them in instruments with high income tax advantages and other benefits such as immediate annuities.

The other groups are usually marketed in one of three ways. The first is the "I'm going to save you money on taxes" approach. The second is the "I'm going to teach you what you need to know to organize your finances" approach. Lastly, the one used least frequently by today's independent advisors is the "I'm going to teach you how to make more money investing" approach.

How do you market to retirees primarily using a tax-based approach? This is often done by branding yourself as a retiree's most trusted tax advisor. You label yourself as a tax expert -- whether you are a C.P.A. yourself or you have a tax specialist on staff. Essential to this form of marketing is access to last year's tax return, which provides a fairly clear picture of your prospect's worth. Often, incentives are offered for discounts on tax preparation as motivation to bring prospects into the office.

Tax-based marketing approaches may also include a promise to find the prospect a way to save money on his or her taxes. The promise is usually validated with a pledge to prepare the tax return free of charge if no savings are found. The beauty of this system is that even though the prospect might not become an advisory client immediately, as a tax-based financial advisor, you have a credible reason to keep bringing the prospect back into your office before each quarterly estimate is due.

Educating prospects on the best way to organize their finances is the most commonly used marketing approach. It is based on a teaching model which explores the features and benefits of the most common financial products and practices. Years ago, this approach was usually carried out by holding a series of classes. Now, it is usually the subject of a single financial seminar. In the seminar, the emphasis is on the advisor's wide range of knowledge of financial strategies related to the accumulation, protection, and distribution of wealth. Even though the stated intent is to educate attendees, the true purpose is to leave the prospect with the feeling that organizing their finances properly is too complicated to accomplish without the services of a financial advisor.

The investment-based approach to financial services marketing is out of favor with many individual advisors, but it still a big lure for those retirees who are under-funded, or are do-it-yourselfers. Ever since the market crash at the beginning of the decade, few advisors or their broker/dealers are willing to take on the risk and liability of promising to beat the markets. The reason this approach still works on certain retirees is because no matter what they say, everyone is still looking for a good stock picker. This is why many investors are still depending on CNBC, magazines, newsletters and Internet sources. In this case, your competition is not in the form of another advisor. Competing sources of financial advice still grab a significant share of your potential client and lead them to do-it-yourself investment options. Of course, the stocks and mutual funds touted in these forums are often subject to extreme volatility and unpredictability. They are the very last place retirees should be turning to for long term investment counsel.

There is an important reason why growth-oriented financial planning is so relevant in today's market. A couple aged 62 now has a one in four chance that at least one of the partners will live to be 98 years old! This fact has profound implications for those working with retirees. Financial planning has usually been divided into three categories: wealth accumulation, wealth protection, and wealth distribution. At retirement, most people are told to stop emphasizing wealth accumulation other than devoting a small portion of their assets to protection against inflation. They also believe they can withdraw a relatively small percentage of their principal annually and remain secure from their greatest fear -- outliving their money. This simply does not apply to today's younger retirees.

If you are marketing to younger retirees with less than $1 million in assets, you are going to have to put wealth accumulation back into your message. According to Robert Arnott, editor of *The Financial Analysts' Journal*, "No major markets are priced to deliver the 5% sustained real rates of return we all seek." Once again, you will have to offer alternative methods to deliver portfolio growth. Of course this growth must be safe and conservative; but it must also be dependable enough to carry your clients well into their 90's. If not, they will have nothing left to protect or distribute.

While all of this sounds most unsettling, unrest among retirees may be good news for advisors who treat their current clients well and focus on more marketing. A VIP Forum entitled "Coming of Age" showed that 23% of retirees expressed a willingness to listen to another advisor's pitch. But there is even better news: 13% of all retirees have switched their advisors in the last 12 months. Obviously the retiree market is still very much open to competition.

# Targeting Baby Boomers

The United States is currently on the cusp of the largest financial revolution in history: the transfer of $11 *trillion* in assets to the 76 million Baby Boomers born between 1946 and 1964.

Many advisors will simply wait until these boomers reach retirement age, and market to them then. This may be a big mistake. As we touched on earlier, this generation will be inheriting unprecedented wealth from their parents in addition to their own accumulated wealth. Many will need the assistance of an advisor to reinvest and manage these assets well before they reach the traditional retirement age. Marketing yourself to the 40-60 age group, as a specialist in the matters that are most likely to affect them, can be a very smart move. If you save boomers money on estate taxes, or perhaps assist with a long-term care policy, they are likely to stay with you as a client through their retirement years. It's an investment that can pay big dividends. But first, financial advisors are going to have a big decision to make, because there are two ways to play this shift in demographics.

From a marketing standpoint, there are options as to how you approach the boomer market. The determining factor could be the demographic makeup of your marketing area. The first option is to market to the affluent, which in this scenario probably means couples with investable assets above $1 million. These are the people who are going to sell highly successful businesses, receive large inheritances and large lump sum retirement stipends with ongoing medical care included. They will be downsizing from expensive homes and dealing with large portfolios funded by their peak earning years.

Overnight, their emphasis (and that of their advisors), will shift from wealth accumulation to wealth management. How these affluent boomers work with financial advisors will become a double-edged sword. People with assets between $1 million and $ 5 million typically work with several advisors concurrently. Because of this, your chance of landing at least some of their business is greater, but you will probably have to settle for just a piece of the pie.

There is another problem as well. These are the clients everybody wants. They are the prime targets of CPAs, attorneys and bankers. It goes without saying if you are going after the highly affluent market, you will need to have a good marketing system in place to distinguish yourself from the competition.

The best hope you have in actually acquiring this type of clientele is that they typically have complex situations at retirement. If you are an expert at solving complex problems, you are much more likely to retain them as clients for a long period of time, (this is the group that reports the least satisfaction with their advisors). And, there is also a greater chance you will win "held away" assets such as IRAs, 401(k)s and brokerage accounts.

There is another advantage to those advisors who are able to make the very wealthy happy. That is the chance to market sophisticated estate planning strategies. For most Boomers, estate planning isn't even on their radar. A recent Harris poll showed that while 22% of current retirees believe they owe their children an inheritance, only 3% of Baby Boomers agree. Perhaps, this is because they feel they are going to need every dime themselves.

If your demographics do not support marketing to the ultra wealthy, you may have to change the way you market to Boomers.

This new generation is going to need a lot of hand-holding. This may become very draining in terms of your time and talent. In the June 2006 issue of *Life & Health Advisor*, author Charles Schewe, Ph.D. says Boomers will require that you pay more attention to back up any product claims you make. And because you will be selling to people who prize holding on to their youth, selling them long-term care plans and disability insurance will be even more difficult because they do not want to face the inevitability of aging.

In the near future, financial planning will look more like life planning. You will need to be an expert in a number of areas such as healthcare, college funding, real estate, income planning, eldercare, Medicaid planning, long term care, and life insurance. You must also be an expert on taxes because they represent 30% of the average household's expenses.

A surprising MetLife survey shows that despite their assumption of eternal health, becoming sick is the chief concern among Baby Boomers. They are terrified of the cost of healthcare and prescription drugs because most Boomer couples have had the experience of becoming the primary caregiver for at least one of the four parents in their family. Boomers need help with this. Demonstrating concern and obtaining detailed knowledge about their parents' affairs can help create a bond with your clients and prospects.

Here are the questions you should ask them: Do you know the location of your parents' wills? Who is their attorney? Who is the executor? Are there provisions for power of attorney in the event of disability? Do you know the extent of your parents' banking, investment, and insurance relationships? Do you have contact with their estate attorney, CPA and all investment advisors? Have you seen their most recent tax return? If so, Boomers know how complicated and expensive old age can be.

While someone age 50 will most likely live 30 more years, they will probably do so with at least one chronic condition. The most common cause of death between ages 50 and 74 is cancer. Many people are surviving cancer, but with the newer treatment modalities they may be spending as much as $40,000 per year out of their own pockets for health care.

Boomers are also increasingly feeling pressure as the "sandwich generation." Not only are they helping to care for their aging parents, but for their adult children as well. Census figures show an extremely high number of 25 to 34 year olds have had to move back home due to the burden of student loans and other consumer debt they have incurred.

The one bright spot in this for advisors would seem to be that while they are working with the parents, they are at the same time meeting and forming a bond with their children who will eventually become clients. So far, the research does not seem to bear this out. Inheritors of wealth typically have their own network of professionals who are closer to themselves in age and with whom they feel more compatible.

When it comes to financial advice, Boomers are notoriously fickle. The consulting firm of McKinsey and Company says 60% of Boomers will have changed advisors at least three times in the 15 years leading up to their retirement. This means any good marketing plan should put a huge emphasis on client retention as well as acquisition.

Part of the problem may be that the financial profession is giving this generation something much different from what they want. When asked what they are looking for, they typically answered: (1) making sure they don't outlive their assets; (2) help in allocating their assets; and (3) help in choosing investments that will perform well. However, when asked about the help they are actually getting from their advisor, Boomers ranked the top three in the opposite order.

There is another important hot button that should be used in marketing to the 40-60 year olds: their overwhelming desire for financial independence. This generation is unique in that in today's tough times they see retirement as a moving target. For the first time in history they will probably spend more in retirement than they did in their final working years. They want an advisor who can create a savings plan that will get them there.

This is also a group which has experienced three major events which have eroded their trust in the economy. The first was the decimation of the markets from 2000 through 2003. The second was the impact of 9/11, and the third is the continuing ethics scandals on Wall Street.

Because the fallacy of promising consistently good returns has been exposed, a new kind of marketing has come into vogue for both the Boomer and retiree. That is the model of financial advisor as therapist. This takes the emphasis off the numbers. It is all about what money means to the prospect emotionally with an emphasis on creating dreams for the future. But financial advisors are not therapists, nor should they be. And whenever the market enters an extended bullish cycle, profit crazed investors may leave these types of advisors for ones who concentrate on delivering returns, even if these returns come in the form of dividends.

There is only one certainty about this dynamic market. More than 70 million Americans are going to really, really need your help. Your future depends on learning how to serve their needs, and if you do, most surely you will find a way to profit by them.

# Targeting the Affluent

There has been no greater influence on how advisors market to the wealthy than a book written by Thomas Stanley and William Danko in 1996 entitled <u>The Millionaire Next Door</u>. In it, the authors describe the wealthy as those who appear to be just like the rest of us except for one overriding characteristic: a mindset diametrically opposed to today's earn-and-consume culture. In other words, don't look for a Mercedes parked in the driveway, but a ten-year-old Chevy.

This theory has lead many advisors to mistakenly believe that prospecting among the wealthy should not be all that different from prospecting among the middle class. But nothing could be further from the truth. Why? Because once potential clients reach a financial threshold of a million dollars or more, they become much more protective about their assets. According to an article entitled, "Top Cats" in the June 2006 issue of *Wealth Manager*, new millionaire prospects become far more skeptical and defensive when approached by advisors who want to manage their money.

Before marketing to the affluent, you need to understand them psychologically. As F. Scott Fitzgerald so famously put it, "The rich are different from you and me." Just how different depends on just how rich they are and how long they have had their money.

Thomas Stanley followed up his seminal book on millionaires, <u>The Millionaire Next Door</u>, with a far more comprehensive study entitled <u>The Millionaire Mind</u>. It contains a chapter called "The Portrait of a Millionaire" which reveals a lot about the very wealthy, and gives clues as to how to market to them:

1. He is a 57 year old male, and the chances are 80% he is still working.

2. Of those who are still working, about 70% earn 80% of their household income, with the rest coming from investments. This household income averages $247,000 per year.

3. Two-thirds are self-employed while only one-fifth of the general population owns their own business. Three-quarters of the millionaire self-employed are entrepreneurs and one-quarter are professionals. This means that with 21% of their wealth still held in their private businesses, their assets will not be entirely available to you.

4. Surprisingly, half of their wives are still working.

5. 80% are college graduates who believe in spending on education much more heavily than the general population. In fact, 55% pay for their children to go to private schools where they are more likely to attend school functions.

6. They are often difficult to reach because two-thirds are at work over 55 hours per week.

7. They invest an average of 20% of their household income every year.

8. 79% have at least one account with a brokerage firm where they hold approximately 20% in transaction securities like stocks and mutual funds, which they rarely sell.

9. They feel their daughters are handicapped in financial earning power compared to their sons, and gift to their children accordingly. However, they are not overwhelmingly concerned with leaving a legacy. In fact many say, "I am my favorite charity."

10. Their average net worth, (exclusive of home), is $3.7 million and 6% have over $10 million. According to a book by J.M. Trippon called How Millionaires Stay Rich Forever, at $10 million in assets their psychological profile begins to

change. They are no longer "the millionaire next door" and are not afraid to indulge in conspicuous consumption.

11. They have lived in the same home for over 20 years and are less likely to downsize at retirement.

12. 80% are first generation affluent. This is highly significant in terms of marketing, as will be discussed later on in the chapter.

13. They have 6.5 times the wealth of their non-millionaire neighbors -- who outnumber them three to one. The difference is that they have chosen to accrue instruments of wealth instead of acquiring material possessions.

14. Their offspring are far less economically productive than they are. In fact there are studies that show 97% of *all* inheritances are spent by the heirs within 18 months.

15. Most relevant is the fact that over 90% of all millionaires with a net worth over $4 million use at least one financial advisor, but report not being very satisfied with them. This may be due in part by the unbelievably low number of in person contacts they get per year from their advisor. 32% report meeting their advisor only once a year, and 30% say they never meet their advisor or broker in person!

According to *Registered Rep* magazine, the ultra wealthy is a rapidly growing group. Their population is increasing at the rate of almost 9% per year. The most staggering statistic of all is that together, they control $91 *trillion* in assets. That is more wealth than the rest of the global population put together!

Millionaires differ not only by the amount of assets they own, but also by how long they have been wealthy. In other words, there truly are differences between new money and old money; and the implications for your marketing are important. The rich are not all alike. It is essential to understand the subtle nuances that distinguish the attitudes and behavior in what is referred to as the "wealth maturation cycle".

Old wealth is more comfortable with money and, therefore, more relaxed about managing it. They are often less skeptical of financial advice; perhaps because they are often well informed. These are the people who grew up affluent, or acquired wealth over a period of time by slowly building their companies or rising to the top of the corporate ladder.

New money is often entrepreneurial, and may have arrived in a single "liquidity event" such as an IPO or the sale of a startup business. These people need more help from a wealth manager. Today's new super-rich grew up lower or middle class. Even those with assets of $5 million plus may still consider themselves middle class at heart. A Worth-Harrison study called "The Status of Wealth in America" shows that only 8% of today's wealthy had wealthy parents.

These are the people classified as "emergents". In order to acquire the newly wealthy or emergents as clients, you need to understand how these people select their advisors, allocate their assets, and plan for the future. Certainly the emergents are the best target for advisors who are looking to build their business with wealthier clients. They haven't yet formed deep relationships with other wealth advisors. But, they want more from you than just advice on investments. Part of your value to these clients is your ability to introduce them to ideas and people who will form their new networks while still maintaining your position as their primary advisor. They are also looking for knowledgeable advisors who can help them make lifestyle choices, such as referrals to luxury goods dealers and high-end realtors. As stated before, networking through CPAs and attorneys works best, but advisors can also get valuable referrals from business valuation specialists, commercial real estate brokers and insurance agents.

Working with emergents also involves the advisor's ability to understand the difference between risk capacity, (the financial capacity to take risks), and risk readiness, (the emotional ability to tolerate risk). People in the early stages of wealth accumulation are much more risk adverse but are willing to increase risk as their portfolios grow. They are not looking for the newest or latest investment ideas, but prefer to grow in measured increments. Never discuss investment vehicles in isolation when marketing to emergents; show them financial products in relation to their overall portfolio goals.

The other two groups of multimillionaires are known as "maturing" or "senior". They are the most difficult to market to because they are the most difficult to access. They have had time to develop networks with other wealthy people. Fortunately, unlike the emergents, they do refer other members of their group to their own advisors.

If you are lucky enough to have clients who qualify, start with them by asking for referrals to friends of theirs who might be interested in your special services. You will not gain their confidence unless you are seen to be one of them. You must fit in by immersing yourself in the activities they are interested in, such as travel, fine wines or various types of collecting. This calls for doing your homework. They are also often active on charitable boards. They have less need than emergents for your contacts, but value new experiences. Look for ways to give them a behind-the-scenes look at something they would normally not have access to when planning an event.

The main challenge faced by advisors who wish to acquire clients with mature wealth, is turning a social situation into an opportunity to acquire their assets. Therefore, it would be considered a terrible faux pas to hand out your business card at a party. A book called The Power of Strategic Intent gives the best advice on prospecting with the clear objective of uncovering serious money. After a bit of small talk, simply say, "Listen, I'd like to run some business ideas by you. How about breakfast or lunch next week?"

This sounds more like you are asking for their advice than asking for their assets. In fact, most will probably be intrigued by the thought of hearing an exciting new idea.

This often works as well because the maturing are more aggressive investors and more open to new opportunities. They have liquidated much of their interest in their own businesses and are diversifying their portfolios across a broader range of investments. They are beginning to think about intergenerational wealth transfer and estate planning. "Seniors" are the classic ultra wealthy who are concerned with distributing their money to future generations and their cherished causes.

If you have set up a true wealth management practice, you and your team of specialists should be able to solve the problems of the affluent and charge them accordingly.

Clearly a consultative approach is a winning one for many advisors, but it doesn't just happen. You must have a systematic practice – one that enables you to create a real partnership between yourself and your clients, a practice that fosters loyalty, referrals and other benefits. By doing so, you should eventually join the ranks of the ultra wealthy yourself.

# Targeting Women

When most advisors say they want to market to women, what they really want is to market to wealthy widows. They have images of doddering ladies left in need of financial guidance after the demise of their husbands. They might also envision widows who are happy to comply with every directive or product suggestion without hesitation or question.

Of course this picture is not entirely accurate -- at least from the woman's point of view. When it comes to their relationships with their advisors, even though they may not display their disapproval openly, in general women are not very happy clients. A study by a major brokerage house in 2004 showed that 79% of all women felt the financial industry treats them with condescension. Women tend to be consensus builders and non-confrontational, so they are less likely than your male clients to let you know when they are dissatisfied with your approach.

This fundamental 'Mars vs. Venus' difference in mentality brings up the question of whether a male advisor should make women his main marketing target. In a study entitled "Building a Niche" in the December 5th issue of *Investment Advisor*, the female author states flatly, "Women want to deal with women."

In truth, men can and should market to women, but it can be difficult for some male advisors. Women in general are far more communicative than most men. Some even expect their advisor to play the additional role of personal confidant at times. How does this even come up? Imagine, for example, a woman making a decision about money regarding her children. She may want to spend more time than a man talking with her advisor about her feelings about each child in her family and how her largesse might affect their degree of ambition later in life. If you are a man of few words or uncomfortable talking about the emotional ramifications of money, you will be ill suited to truly meet the needs of women as your primary target.

In order to attract women as clients, you may need to hold events that are particularly suited only to a female audience. For example, consider targeting wealthy female prospects with an invitation to high tea accompanied by a fashion show or perhaps a spa day. The strategy is viable but most male advisors will need the help of their wives or a female assistant to pull it off successfully.

If you market through seminars, you need to be aware that women do not like to go out in the evening alone. Dinners usually outdraw lunches for general public seminars. But when marketing specifically to women, lunches draw better than dinner events. Make sure to offer at least one lunch session on your invitation.

If you do decide to specialize in marketing to women, you also need to make sure your approach is not based upon the inaccurate stereotype that women are financially illiterate. In other words, you should market to women with the same degree of sophistication that you market to men. The trick lies in finding women with sufficient wealth to make targeting them worth your while.

Because of the huge disparity between women and men in earning power, the dividing line seems to be whether or not female prospects are, or ever were, married. Although not impossible, it is extremely difficult for women in our society to build assets on their own unless they have inherited money and are investing it wisely. Therefore, most advisors direct their efforts to well-to-do divorcees and widows. What they fail to realize is that married women may need to be addressed apart from their husbands. Almost all advisors refuse to meet with a married woman who shows up at an appointment solo. This is an unwise practice, because in these days of frequent second marriages, there are many women who wish to manage sums of money from divorce settlements -- or sometimes an inheritance -- totally apart from the controlling influence of their spouse. The problem for married women with assets, which they wish to keep exclusively their own, is that in meetings with advisors, the men tend to totally dominate the discussion. Wives may sit through an entire appointment remaining grudgingly silent for fear of embarrassing their husband in front of their advisor. There is also a sizeable group of women who have never married. Some may still have substantial assets due to an inheritance, climbing the corporate ladder, or owning a successful business. Never turn away a potential client because she comes in alone.

Even when women appear to be totally dependent on their husband's assets, they may well be the primary financial decision maker behind the scenes. Over the years of the marriage, they may have handled the budgeting and the bill paying. They might be the person with the greater grasp of what it is going to take for them to live comfortably in retirement. Make sure you spend equal time talking with each spouse. And make sure you do so in the same tone of voice with the same financial vocabulary, unless you are directly asked to simplify by one spouse or the other.

Problems in marketing to females don't occur only in the office. *Senior Market Advisor* sponsored a discussion group at their annual expo about targeting women, and they got an earful. One irate woman vented her frustration this way: "I would say there is a big difference between marketing to women and marketing to men. We get stuff in the mail from advisors that is addressed to my husband, but I make a lot of the decisions in my house. Include me. Don't assume the man makes all the decisions just because we're seniors."

Oddly, there is a phenomenon that seems to occur among women when they hit their mid-fifties. They begin to save and budget for the future with increased zeal, while their husbands are usually less concerned. What lies behind the discrepancy between men and women in their mid-fifties? Women are painfully aware of the difference in mortality statistics. Even wealthy women fear that the death of their husband may leave them alone and penniless.

When crafting your marketing message, lifelong financial security should be at the forefront. Whether through death or divorce, women secretly fear abandonment. They are looking to form a bond with an advisor who can assure them they won't wind up on Medicaid in a nursing home. Aside from being an expert at monitoring investments and ensuring sufficient cash flow, you will also need to be well versed in the area of healthcare options. They need to know that no matter what the future brings, there will be someone who will ensure they will be well cared for. They also know from horror stories that abound in the media and among their friends that they may not be able to depend upon their children.

Just how do you go about finding women with sufficient investable assets of their own? Targeting women is simple with direct mail marketing. Most list sources offer the ability to select female heads of household by age and income. Direct mail is the only way to reach this market exclusively in a cost efficient manner.

Your professional referral network is an excellent way to obtain female clients. The most obvious source is through strategic alliances with divorce and estate attorneys. In fact, a whole new specialty of divorce mediation by financial advisors now exists. It is represented by three different professional organizations which offer special designations and give referrals to their members.

You will also want to introduce yourself to grief counselors at local funeral homes. Provide them with material on what to do financially -- in both emotional and practical terms -- upon the death of a spouse. This kind of pamphlet can be a springboard for monthly meetings, or it can be given out to funeral directors who may encounter a widow or widower who needs your help. It goes without saying that this approach must be done with the utmost discretion and subtlety.

Oppenheimer Funds, Inc. determined that women are at least half-owners of nearly 50% of all private U.S. firms. Female entrepreneurs represent a huge market for financial advisors. Again, direct mail is the best way to target this market. Your list provider can help you locate a list of female owned businesses in your area. Your Chamber of Commerce directory may also be a useful tool.

Most cities hold a women's expo at least once a year. Consider getting a booth to position yourself as an expert in women's financial issues. Market yourself not only to the attendees, but make the rounds of the other booths as well. You can also mail an invitation to a targeted list of women in your area. Let them know your booth location and offer them a free consultation for stopping by. The odds are favorable that you will be the only person there marketing services in your field.

There are also almost always women's clubs and professional organizations, such as 'women in media', which meet monthly. Again, ask the program chairman for the chance to address the group on a topic which will affect them, such as retirement plan funding.

If you are marketing to women, you have two excellent role models whose approach resonates with them. Both are quite famous for their ability to relate to the needs of women. One is author Suze Orman of PBS fundraising telethon fame, and the other is Jean Chatsky of *Money* magazine and a frequent guest on the *Today Show* and *Oprah*. They take a no nonsense approach to saving and investing. They know how to empower women without using the clichéd 'superwoman' imagery so common to most financial advertising aimed at women.

The approach used by Orman and Chatsky is based on the way women are used to running their own households. It is grounded in practicality. Their genius lies in demystifying money management. You may emulate their methods and approach, but you may want to avoid recommending their books or articles to your clients, as both advise women to be extremely wary of financial advisors.

When marketing to women, resist the temptation to try to frighten them into doing business with you. Studies show women respond much better to a positive approach. While fear may spur a man into action, it may cause a woman to freeze. Take a positive and supportive approach in terms of their knowledge base as well. Let your prospective client know she can ask you any question at all, and she will never appear stupid.

Marketing to women requires concentration on the unique nature of female psychology when it comes to money. Female clients and prospects may need specialized handling, but it's crucial that you don't appear as though you are treating them differently. The most important thing is to avoid condescension. For the advisor who is oriented towards long term consultative relationships, nothing could be more rewarding than working with women because you will probably be regarded with true appreciation if you help them build the security they desire.

# Turning Targets
# Into Prospects

# Publicity & Public Relations

The practice of proactively promoting your business through publicity and advertising is just one of the activities you must pursue to build your reputation and establish credibility. The earlier a financial advisor does this in his career, the better. Once you've earned your credentials through public relations, you can refer to them over and over again for decades. You are looking for the opportunity to add phrases like "As seen on CNN" or "has appeared in the *Financial Times*" when you are introduced before a seminar or are constructing a bio for your brochure.

The reason a publicity campaign is a finite endeavor rather an on-going one is quite simple. It will greatly enhance your reputation as a member of the elite in your field, but it will almost never directly bring you clients. As an example, there is a financial planner who, with the help of a public relations firm, managed to appear on CNBC a total of 16 times. While this accomplishment brought incalculable value to his resume, he did not receive a single phone call from a prospect as a result of all that television exposure.

Even so, every independent advisor should construct a publicity campaign as part of his marketing plan. There is no better way, (including professional designations), to establish yourself with the public as the recognized financial expert in your community. The level at which you concentrate your efforts depends upon your target audience. There is a big difference between impressing retirees attending a dinner seminar and publicity aimed at the acquisition of multi-millionaire CEOs as your clients. However, it never hurts to aim as high as possible.

Any way you approach it, getting publicity depends on one thing, either being or hiring an extraordinary writer who is skilled at creating newsworthy hooks that will entice the media. If you don't have the time or possess the talent to do this yourself, but can afford a minimum of $1000/month for at least six months, there is an option available to you. The Public Relations Society of America has a "green book" that lists PR specialists in the financial arena. In this case you are buying not only a writer but someone with highly placed contacts as well. To make sure this person is genuine, ask to see tear sheets of the stories written and placed in recognized media outlets for an advisor whose practice is similar to your own.

No matter which media you are targeting, you are going to need someone skilled at writing compelling cover letters, press releases and feature articles. This writer is not going to be a financial advisor, so you will be required to provide the basis of the content. You should keep abreast of the stories covered by the publications, in which you wish to appear, so you have a good idea of the kind of article and style they are looking for.

Although it might sound extreme, there is one surefire way to enhance your chances of getting publicity. Become an author of a financial book. If writing isn't your strong suit, or you can't devote the time, consider hiring a writer to assist you.

The cost to self-publish a 100-page paperback book, (which is all you need), at a quantity of 1,000 should run $5 - $10 per book, plus your writer's fee. You will want to get an ISBN number so your book can be listed on sites such as *Amazon.com*. Although writing and publicizing a book sounds like an overwhelming endeavor, this can be the best marketing money you will ever spend, because nothing conveys expertise like the word "author".

As the author of your own financial book, editors at newspapers and magazines and program directors at radio and television stations are more likely to entertain your publicity proposals.

It should be obvious that the goal of this chapter is to get you to aim high and garner credentials from the national media even though your marketing focus is local. During the period of your publicity campaign, you will have to keep abreast of what is going on in the financial news in the major media. While the possibilities of placing an article in the *Wall Street Journal* or *USA Today* are slim to nonexistent, you can still get published in these newspapers or prestigious magazines simply by writing a letter to the editor or an op-ed column. The key is to e-mail an imaginatively worded contrarian response to the relevant story the very same day it appears. If it does indeed get printed, you have your credential from that publication.

The same approach goes for the national cable news channels such as CNN, Fox, CNBC, Bloomberg, and MSNBC. One particularly astute advisor responded to a comment by a famous anchor on MSNBC about the US economy, and wound up doing an on air telephone interview with him. In that case, something as simple as a phone call brought him a major league credential.

If your broker dealer will allow it, you can also leverage the Internet to obtain an impressive title. You should never depend on your regular business website to generate clients or publicity. It is mostly a means of communicating with existing clients. However, if you are a specialist in a field such as Long Term Care or College Funding, you can become the president of a dotcom with a name based upon your specialty. There are times that spending $35 for a relevant domain name and perhaps $20 a month for web hosting will give you a credential that can open a lot of doors.

If you don't have the time or inclination to monitor news sources on a constant basis even for a few months, there is another respected method that can be used to garner national attention. It is known as the *PR Newswire*. It is considered reliable and universal because its releases are frequently picked up by Yahoo News and Microsoft's MSN News. If you have a thought provoking or topical press release, it may be worth spending the $150 - $180 fee to put out a news release statewide, with a good chance of getting picked up nationally as well. You will enhance your chances further if you pay for a priority listing.

The same company also maintains a relatively inexpensive clipping service that will send you copies of any story mentioning you. Obviously you will want to maintain a file because you can use these stories in seminar marketing handouts, or even frame them on your office walls. Remember, media exposure won't drive clients to your door; but it definitely enhances your image and credibility with your prospects.

For those who wish to be considered for national radio and television shows, (which can be done by remote from your own location), there are three guides to choose from: Bradley's Guide to the Top National TV Talk and Interview Shows, Bacon's Media Directories, and The Yearbook of Experts. You will need to send a press kit to the producer or booking agent of the shows that interest you. Your press kit does not have to be fancy, but it should look as though it comes from a national public relations firm, so we would suggest not using the name of your financial advisory firm as the contact. Your press kit should contain a bio with a list of all relative accomplishments, a professional head shot, a one page cover letter that describes why you should be booked on the show, a list of 7-10 intriguing questions that the interviewer might want, (but without the answers), a copy of all articles by or about you, and a description of your book if you have written one.

So far, the emphasis has been placed on garnering national credentials that will give you prestige. But no matter how affluent your target market is, you need to work the local publicity and advertising angle as well. Basically, advertising is paid publicity. And no matter what the ad salesmen tell you, there are relatively few conditions where it is truly worth the expenditure for financial advisors. The urge for caution comes from the fact that advertising contracts usually are built upon the premise that you need to place ads over and over again in order to gain name recognition.

Some publications offer a hybrid ad that is known as an "advertorial". Basically, it is an ad that is written and laid out like a genuine news or feature story. The story should not appear to be written by you but about you. Not all magazines will accept advertorials, so you need to start by contacting their advertising director. Unfortunately this can be an expensive proposition because you will be paying full page ad rates for at least one or two pages.

The value from this type of advertising comes not from your one time appearance in the magazine, but from the reprints they generate. A reprint should consist of the cover page of the magazine reproduced exactly as it appeared on the newsstands. Your advertorial should combine the inside contents with your contact information displayed on the back page. First, bargain with the magazine itself to see if they will throw in any free reprints. You also need to make sure they will give you a PDF file of the cover and the advertorial itself --as it appeared in the magazine -- so you can produce additional reprints yourself.

There are other less costly forms of publicity on the local level. In the past, some advisors have done well by creating and hosting their own weekly radio shows. The beauty of a radio show is that even in a fairly large media market, a one hour show can be quite inexpensive to produce. Using a weaker signal station in a local market, you can do a mid-day show for a few hundred dollars in production costs. You will be expected to find your own sponsors, but considering the low production costs, all you need is two or three sponsors to completely underwrite your show.

You will also be expected to put together a program proposal that covers the station demographics and reach, as well as a full description of your show. One real benefit may come from using your show as a forum for inviting and interviewing guests whom you would like to have in your circle of influence; or even as potential clients. You may also find that they will advertise their appearance on your show and thereby bring you more listeners.

Then there is television. You can create and find sponsors for a local cable show in much the same way as radio. However, you will be expected to submit a project proposal to the station. This will first entail a project description consisting of a synopsis and treatment. For advice on how to do this, visit the Independent Television Service website at *www.itvs.org/producers/treatment.html*.

You will also need to create a project timetable, budget, and list of personnel for a television program. Your chances of being accepted will increase if you can show evidence of interactive elements, such as a companion website. Remember that the value here is not in obtaining clients, but in leveraging your guest list and obtaining a television credential. Never let the public know that you are the host of an obscure cable show. Always refer to the station by its call letters and not by its channel number, which will usually sound less impressive.

Advisors who are independent and not bound by compliance departments can appear on regular local television newscasts because they don't need to get clearance before commenting on the air. Certainly with television news and even newspapers, time is of the essence. You should develop and maintain a relationship with a reporter and/or the assignment editor at the stations in your area. Let them know you are available for interviews on financial stories at a moment's notice.

It is not difficult. Simply phone the news director and ask if you can send them a press packet that they can keep on standby. Include a letter which lists your contact information and some suggestions for evergreen financial stories they can pre-tape and use as fillers on slow news days.

Television talk shows are a completely different matter. Their timetable is much, much longer. At a minimum, talk shows usually book at least six weeks in advance. Here is where being the author of a book really helps, because show producers need strong justification for putting you on the air. Talk shows are looking for intriguing five or six minute segments that contain visual elements whenever possible, instead of what they refer to as "talking heads". The best approach here is to contact the show's producer. Volunteer to appear on a national holiday when it is almost impossible for the producer to find guests. Remember, even though most of the audience may be tuned into the Rose Bowl Parade or a football game on another channel, you have still managed to rack up another credential.

Also keep in mind that no matter how many professional designations you may have, the public is more likely to remember your media credentials. The right kind of publicity truly distinguishes you from your less savvy, lower profile competition.

# Existing Clients

There are two basic types of marketing, internal and external. Internal marketing is usually referred to as client referrals, and advisors love it to a fault. In fact, most advisors say that client referrals are their main source of new prospects.

What's so wrong with that? Nothing if you are a major firm. The problem lies in the fact that you have to reach critical mass to make referrals viable as your only form of marketing. Given that the average referral rate for all advisors comes from a mere 11% of their client base, you are not going to grow your business in a significant enough way through referrals alone. In fact, you may even be losing ground when you factor in a normal attrition rate. You need to enhance those numbers. You need to market.

Certainly, referrals are an integral part of any marketing plan. You need to have a disciplined process that enhances your ability to source business from your existing clients. And almost every referral process begins with identifying exactly which kinds of clients you would like more of. But before you get busy with your exercise in cloning, you need to make sure your "A" list clients are as happy with you as you are with them.

Not surprisingly, client loyalty stems as much from the attention they get as it does on investment returns. The number of "touches" or contacts the average client gets from an advisor is 14 per year. Even though many of these are fairly meaningless contacts, such as generic client correspondence, 14 touches are enough to keep most people in your stable -- and to bring you a few referrals. But try to think of your clients in a completely different way. Think of how you can turn them into a powerful sales force.

Again, you have to start by making sure your clients are not just happy, but downright *ecstatic* over you and your service. *Investment Advisor*, June 2006, suggests conducting a survey asking the following questions:

- What is the client's level of overall satisfaction with the advisor?
- What is the level of satisfaction with the administrative team?
- What are the clients' expectations regarding frequency of contact?
- Is there interest in or need for additional products and services?
- What share of the clients' portfolio do you have?
- What single factor is most important to the client?
- Is the client willing to refer others to the advisor?

You can do the survey yourself; it should not require the assistance of an outside firm. Limit your survey to a maximum of 10 questions. Structure the questions so that your clients can respond using a 5 point Likert scale. Avoid open-ended questions that require clients to write a narrative. This requires too much of their time, and will result in a poor response to your survey; making the responses difficult to quantify for your analysis.

If you do conduct this survey yourself, have the responses go to an address or PO Box other than your office. Instead of your practice name, use something generic like "Survey Opinion Poll". Never put your client's name on the survey. If they think the responses will be seen by you, they may not answer truthfully, and your results will be skewed. Instead, assign each client a unique 5-digit ID number, and inconspicuously print the corresponding code on each client's survey. While your primary purpose is to get an aggregate sense of your clientele's satisfaction, being able to identify individual responses can help you improve those specific relationships.

If you construct the questions so they are answered by circling a number between 1 and 5, (with 5 being the highest), 4.6 would indicate an average level of satisfaction. If your overall score is 3 or below, you are not only at risk of losing clients, you do not have a satisfaction level that will yield a successful referral network.

Perhaps the most important question on the survey is the one which addresses the question of how often clients expect to meet with you in person. *Advisor Impact* did a study on this subject. It shows that the greatest number (32%) of people with less than $500,000 expected to meet with their advisor twice a year. However, those with assets above that figure expected to meet quarterly.

One of the most common methods of obtaining referrals is to ask for them by sending out a letter. Sometimes the letter focuses on another topic, but referral cards are included in the envelope. If you use the standard referral letter that is part of so many customer relations management systems, you can expect to receive a return of about 10%. You are going to need something more explicit to raise your numbers. An excellent example of a meaningful letter comes from an article entitled "From Tactical to Practical" by Larry Chambers in the November, 2005 issue of *Investment Advisor*. As printed in the magazine, it would be far too cumbersome for any client to wade through. Therefore, the version presented here has been shortened considerably but still maintains the essence of what you want to say:

Dear Client,

From time to time clients have sent me referrals, for which I am deeply grateful. My goal is to treat every person you send me with respect, honesty, and dignity. I would like to give you an idea of the guidelines I use in dealing with anyone you refer to me.

1. We begin by listening to what the person you referred to us tells us what they are trying to accomplish. We often do this by providing a questionnaire.
2. We set target goals which are dollar amounts the prospective client desires to reach at some point in the future if all goes well. We also set fallback goals, which is the minimum a client must have in the future.
3. We do some fine tuning to focus on the investment strategy that has the highest probability of achieving the desired result.
4. We optimize the allocation of investment styles between taxable and tax-deferred portfolios.
5. We create an investment policy statement which reveals all costs and fees.
6. If needed, we conduct an investment manager search. Rest assured that anyone we recommend has gone through an extensive screening process.
7. We follow up on a quarterly basis with meetings and detailed reports of their progress.

I feel my investment process is what sets me apart from the competition. I hope this letter helps you understand what happens when you send a friend or associate to us. Please don't hesitate to contact me if you have any questions.

Very truly yours,
Financial Advisor

While you probably don't want to duplicate this letter in its entirety because you may follow a very different process, what you do want to duplicate is the fact that it will grab your clients' attention, and plant the seed for future referrals. The letter doesn't overtly ask for a referral. Instead it assumes the client will refer you and implies that if they have not yet referred you, they should.

It shows that you have taken a great deal of time and attention in order to convey your true methodology in achieving your objective of gaining more clients through referrals. This is a letter that could only be sent by someone who holds the highest professional standards. This is the kind of letter that deserves a response.

While many clients will simply send you a list of names and phone numbers, this is not what you are looking for because all it will amount to is a barely warm call. What you need is action in the form of an introduction. Not only do you need an introduction; you need an endorsement. You want your client to tell the referral exactly how you have helped him or her. How do you work this to your best advantage?

All referrals, both personal and professional, should be followed up three times.

1.  Within one day of the conversation, express gratitude for the referral and ensure your prompt action. For example, simply say, "I just wanted to call you and thank you for referring me to Mr. Jones. I will do everything I can to make sure he pays the minimum in taxes as we have done with you." Also let the referring party know that you will not make the contact until you have been notified that the referral has actually been made.

2.  After you have contacted the person to whom you were referred, send a status report and say thanks again. "I

have spoken with Mr. Jones. You were right; he is a terrific person, and I will do all I can to help him."

3. If you get the referral as a client, send a personal thank you note to your client.

What has been described above is the bare minimum. There is a way to ensure even more referrals. Invite your referring client and spouse along with your new client and spouse out for a nice dinner. This is both a welcome and a thank you. If you take this extra step, you are effectively training both parties to refer additional prospects to you. And by the way, don't forget to mention this referral practice in your personal newsletter, a publication that you should be sending out quarterly.

Aside from asking for referrals, you should also be soliciting testimonials, because they provide both intellectual and emotional validation. This is somewhat trickier than asking for a referral in a letter. Many clients will have a difficult time constructing exactly what to say, even if it is just a paragraph. Many will agree to help and then ask you what they should say. Engage them in conversation on the subject and extract some quotes from the conversation. Then ask for permission to use those quotations. Of course, you should never use *any* testimonial without clearing it with the client beforehand.

It is essential to include these testimonials in all your marketing materials. Be sure to scatter them throughout instead of presenting them all in one place, because you never know what parts of your marketing materials your prospects are actually reading. You can also capture video testimonials and use them on your website or at a seminar.

Another dependable source of referrals is the use of advisory councils. They provide you with an opportunity to tap into the collective thoughts of a group of your top clients. These should be people who genuinely enjoy being a sounding board, mentoring, and acting as a referral source. While the whole concept of asking clients to help you build your business may seem presumptuous, most will be flattered.

Of course you are looking for clients who are centers of influence; but the composition of your advisory council must be diversified as well. Even though it is tempting to pick only high profile members, you should also recruit highly social employees from major corporations too. Choose anywhere from six to eight members, and limit them to a one year term. This way you get to utilize the contacts of more of your best clients. At the outset, let them know that you want them to be brutally honest. If your advisory council members provide you with frank advice, they can save you from making costly marketing mistakes. Four meetings a year should probably be the maximum, and each should be amply rewarded for their participation. You might give them a plaque for their participation, as well as gift certificates for a round of golf, or a fine dinner they can enjoy with their spouse.

Without a doubt, one of the most common methods of obtaining referrals, is by holding a client dinner and asking your clients to bring a friend. In some cases this method yields tangible results; but generally these events turn into little more than client appreciation parties. To get better results, don't just send out invitations, but also call your top clients and enlist their help. However, even this is often not enough. Here is where you need to become more inventive. Think of an occasion that is either a learning event or something out of the ordinary. You might want to hire a golf pro to give a one hour clinic, then set up a round of golf in which you pay for your clients if they bring two or three friends. Be sure to cap the game off by socializing over a round of drinks.

Another opportunity to gain referrals from your clients is to educate them – and their friends. Ask some of your top clients what financial topics they would like to learn more about. Then conduct three or four workshops a year to cover those topics. Make sure they know they are invited to bring someone who might also be interested. You may invite an estate planning attorney or a CPA to increase workshop attendance. Just make sure everyone in the audience recognizes you as the architect of all things financial.

There is a new school of thought in referral marketing that could be referred to as "the exclusive club" technique. Even though it is outlined here for your information, that does not imply an endorsement of this kind of approach. Basically the advisor tells his prospects that he has room to take on only a very limited number of new clients each year. He is so busy attending to their portfolios that he has no time for marketing. In order to become a client, a prospect has to qualify.

Part of the qualification process is a written agreement that if all service goals are met, each year the new client will refer a certain number of prospects. The number is usually between two and four. The rationale is that this process frees up the advisor to spend all his time helping his clients reach their financial goals, instead of searching for new business.

This technique is inherently risky. Aside from the arrogance of this approach, it seems fundamentally wrong. An advisor should never ask for referrals too soon in a relationship, because it takes time to build trust. You also need to make sure you aren't asking for referrals too often. You don't want to look desperate. Also, it will eventually cause your client to wonder if you are putting more emphasis on marketing than on tending to his account.

The real key to referral marketing is to constantly vary the ways in which you ask your clients for their help in acquiring new business.

Take out a calendar and develop a personal referral program just as you would any other marketing program. If you already have highly satisfied clients, you should certainly do much better than the average advisor. Once you have perfected client marketing, you are ready to turn your attention to marketing through professionals.

# Other Professionals

Many financial advisors don't actively seek referrals from other professionals, but they certainly should. According to the October 2005 issue of *Selling Power*, over 50% of referrals that come from other professionals result in the prospect becoming a client. The reasons are twofold. First, this method shows your potential client that you are someone who can be trusted. Second, it lets the prospect know that talking with you is definitely worth their time.

Unfortunately, gaining professional referrals is not easy because the main sources of referrals -- attorneys and CPAs -- are constantly besieged with requests from financial advisors seeking their referrals. To overcome this reluctance, you need to expand your base for referral sources. Don't just limit yourself to CPAs and attorneys; include other professions as well.

Any profession that sees money in motion is potentially a good source of referrals. Examples include real estate agents, insurance brokers, homebuilders, luxury auto dealers, bankers, funeral directors, and architects. While referrals from these other sources may not carry the same weight as a referral from a trusted attorney or CPA, they are certainly worth exploring.

There is another relatively new profession that will be eager to partner with you. These are career counselors and coaches. Career development professionals often see financial fears as the main roadblock to clients' optimizing their true career goals. They know their clients cannot think about the future rewards of a job change or retirement if they are worried about how they are going to pay the bills.

You might even consider including career asset management as part of your financial planning process. After all, earned income will probably constitute the greatest source of your clients' investment dollars. It makes sense to refer some of your clients to a well-qualified career counselor who may be able to help him or her secure a job that pays more money. You will both benefit from the client's success.

Certainly the best referral source is a client's accountant. CPAs are regarded as the most trusted advisor by the vast majority of people. Unfortunately many advisors have wasted a great deal of time and money trying to win the approval of accountants to no avail; either by wining and dining them or by sharing the stage with them at seminars. The best method is a simple one. Begin by asking each of your clients to give you the name and address of their CPA. Your next step should be to send them a letter like this:

Dear CPA:

As you may know, I am working as the financial advisor for your client, John Smith. You will be receiving the paperwork pertinent to any possible transactions, before they occur, so we may get your input on the tax ramifications. Our office will also send you a copy of all additional paperwork regarding your client.

I would be more than happy to meet with you in person if you feel it might be of benefit to Mr. Smith. In the meantime, I look forward to working with you. Please let me know if there is any way I can be of assistance.

Very truly yours,
Financial Advisor

Notice that the key to this letter is to refer to Mr. Smith always as the *CPA's client*, not your own. This would also hold true during the course of any meeting. You might not exactly feel that way, but the wording is an important acknowledgment of the accountant's professional pride. The other key to this approach is showing yourself to be a professional eager to work with other financial professionals in the best interest of your clients. Even if this letter does not bring about immediate referrals, it will keep the CPA from saying something derogatory about you to the client. This can be extremely important during a down market. If you do follow up and maintain contact as promised with the CPA, you stand a much-improved chance of obtaining referrals.

The second best referral source is attorneys. Because most financial advisors are also involved to some degree in estate planning; that opens the door to direct contact with your client's attorney. Speak to your client about their estate plans and follow up by calling for an in person meeting with their lawyer. Or, you can send a letter similar to the CPA letter above. Again, always refer to the client as the attorney's client. It is a professional courtesy that costs you nothing and could pay off by making the attorney an ally and a potential source of referrals.

In the previous chapter on personal referrals, there was a mention of holding educational seminars. You should use these as an opportunity to meet professionals by asking them to speak to your clients and their friends. Hopefully, they will see this as a way to expand their own client base as well. Don't forget the distinction. You should never share the stage at a seminar held for new prospects. But, inviting non-competing professionals to take part in events with your own clients can definitely pay off.

Another option is to ask desired professionals to write a brief article for your newsletter or website. If they balk at the work involved, simply ask for permission to do a brief interview with them instead. Make sure they receive a copy of what you have written for review before it is published.

The key to this professional referral strategy is never to expect a referral without giving something in return. With top professionals, you are going to have to do the giving first. Some financial advisors have even set aside office space where an attorney or CPA can work with mutual clients. If you have the spare space, consider how many contacts you can derive from inviting other professionals to use your office as an additional branch. Unfortunately, you may find that you are the one who does all the giving. If you do not receive a referral after a maximum of three months, it is time to consider politely severing the relationship.

There is another referral marketing strategy at your disposal, albeit a more costly one. You can offer to throw a client appreciation party for the attorney or CPA. It may sound unorthodox, but you will likely gain a number of personal introductions at the event. Obviously, you can't be seen trying to drum up business at this kind of affair, and you probably won't get any new clients immediately. But at the very least, you may be able to add the guests to your database as future prospects.

Finally, try to speak to pertinent professional organizations at one of their monthly meetings. Contact the program director and suggest at least five intriguing topics that are directly applicable to their profession. After the event, try to gather as many business cards as you can and thank all the attendees and the person who booked you. This is also the time to ask the program director for a testimonial comment in writing. A testimonial will make the next speaking opportunity easier to obtain.

As you can see, gaining clients through professional referrals is no easy task. But just like publicity campaigns and client referrals, a professional referral campaign should be considered an essential component of every marketing plan.

# Direct Mail

The marketing methods we have discussed to this point certainly all have places in your arsenal. But simply stated, *there is no better way to rapidly grow a financial advisory practice than through the ongoing use of direct mail.* The other techniques focus mainly on image and/or relationship building – both important to be sure. But when it comes to generating new prospects – *lots* of new prospects – nothing beats direct mail.

Why is direct mail so effective for financial advisors? The main reason is targeting. No other form of advertising gives you the ability to precisely target your prospects like direct mail. As a financial advisor, you are only marketing to one or two specific segments of the population. Other forms of advertising, such as Newspapers and TV, have a broad distribution. You can't control who sees your message; yet you pay for every person who will even *potentially* see your promotion.

To illustrate, picture yourself in a stadium filled with every single resident of your marketing area; young and old, rich and poor. When you advertise in the newspaper, or on radio and TV, you're paying to reach each and every one of those people in your market, even though the vast majority of them don't fit your ideal customer profile.

Now, ask all of those under the age of 55 to leave the stadium. Suddenly more than half of the stadium is empty. Next, ask everyone with a household income of less than $75,000 to leave. Out of the 50,000 people you started with, the crowd has now been reduced and refined to 5,000. All the people remaining are your prime prospects, pre-qualified by age and income.

In essence, you are doing the same thing with a well-targeted mailing campaign. If you only want to reach 10% of the people in your market, why pay for the other 90%? Doesn't it make sense to deliver your message only to the people you want to see it? That is the targeting power that direct mail gives you.

Direct mail is also one of the most cost efficient advertising media. When comparing advertising costs, it is important to understand the pricing methods and terminology. Most advertising is sold on the basis of "cost per thousand", (CPM). Basically, it is the amount of money you spend to reach (potentially) 1,000 people. Based solely on CPM, direct mail appears more expensive than other forms of advertising.

But the important number to look at is cost per *response*. For example, let's say you can place an ad in a newspaper with a circulation of 150,000 for $1,250.The CPM for that newspaper ad is $8.33 ($1250 ÷ 150), however, your actual CPM is going to be as much as 100 times higher. You see, although 150,000 copies get distributed; only a small percentage of the readers will actually look at your ad. An even smaller percentage will be age and income qualified. See the calculation below:

|  |  |  |
|---|---|---|
|  | 150,000 | copies of the newspaper |
| x | 20% | people who read the page where your ad appears |
|  | **30,000** | |
| x | 50% | who actually notice your ad on that page |
|  | **15,000** | |
| x | 50% | who notice your ad and meet your target age |
|  | **7,500** | |
| x | 20% | who also meet your target income |
|  | **1,500** | **who notice your ad *and* are qualified** |
| ÷ | **$1,250** | **(cost of ad)** |
|  | **$833** | **Your actual CPM** |

By contrast, let's assume you can send 5,000 direct mail pieces to an age and income qualified list for $2,500. Your CPM is $500 period – no guessing. Not only is direct mail more cost effective, your message and offer won't get thrown out with the daily news. You also have the ability to address your prospect personally, which enhances your response.

If your newspaper ad gets your offer in front of 1,500 viable prospects and generates a 2% response, you will receive about 30 calls. If your direct mail piece generates the same 2% response, you would receive 100 calls. Based on those numbers, your newspaper ad yields a cost per response (CPR) of $41.67, ($1,250 ÷ 30), while your direct mail campaign delivered a prospect for $25 each, ($2,500 ÷ 100). Cost Per Response is the only way to truly measure your marketing costs.

Before we get into the details of putting together a successful direct mail campaign for your own practice, please take the following advice to heart: **Use a professional direct mail company that specializes in financial marketing.** Why is this so critical? A direct mail campaign requires knowledge of graphic design, copywriting, paper stock, printing, bindery, list providers, data processing, postal regulations, automation discounts, barcodes and much more. Mistakes or oversights can literally cost you thousands of dollars.

Think for a moment about the services you provide to your own clients. Theoretically, they could pick and trade their own stocks online, transfer their 401(k) money into a CD at the bank, and get their long-term care insurance from a local agent. Why do they need you?

Because you know what you're doing, that's why. You are an experienced professional who helps your clients avoid costly mistakes and achieve their financial goals. Direct mail professionals do the same for you. Building a bird feeder is a do-it-yourself project. Creating and executing an effective direct mail campaign is not.

Your direct mail company should also offer proven, pre-tested marketing materials that have been successful for other advisors. This is another very big advantage to working with a professional marketing company. You recommend investment strategies and products to your clients because you know from experience that they have worked for others. Shouldn't you follow your own advice and seek out marketing programs that are proven performers?

With that said, here are a few things to consider when hiring a direct mail company. Get actual printed samples of their work. Everything looks pretty good on a website. You want to be able to hold a sample in your hand and examine the work closely. Is the color sharp and true? Is the copywriting compelling? Does the overall package project an image of quality? You want your marketing material to position you as an established, caring professional.

Go over your campaign goals with the mail company and ask for their advice and recommendations. Your direct mail representative should be more than an order taker. The focus should be on your results rather than the size and price of your order. This could be the beginning of a long and profitable partnership for both of you. If you feel like you are getting a high pressure sales pitch, you probably are. You won't get that from a reputable firm.

Of all the elements of a direct mail campaign, the mailing list is the most important. You can have the greatest offer in the world, but if it isn't reaching the right people, your response will suffer – in quantity, quality, or both. If you are working with a professional direct mail company, the use of their mailing list is usually included in the price of the project. There are five major list compilers in the U.S. All provide good quality lists, but each has their strengths and weaknesses. There are literally thousands of list brokers, resellers and lettershops who are licensed to sell this data as well. However, their levels of expertise – especially pertaining to financial offers – vary greatly. So do their prices. Again, partnering with a direct mail company that specializes in financial marketing is critical. Not only will they have access to all the major list suppliers, they will also know which has the best data for your particular offer. For example, "Compiler A" may have more precise age targeting, whereas "Compiler B" may offer more accurate income models. If your offer is for people who will turn 65 this year, you will want to use Compiler A. If you are trying to target ultra wealthy investors, you may want to use Compiler B. Your direct mail vendor has a vested interest in helping you select the right list and list provider, and should offer a choice of counts and prices from different sources.

When choosing the parameters of the mailing list, you will be asked to pick the zip codes, the age range, and the estimated income of the prospects you want to target. Each of these items is called a "filter". There are other filters you can add, such as marital status, home value, ethnicity, investable assets and on and on. But don't overdo it. Not only does each filter add to the cost, but you can actually over target and end up excluding good potential prospects. The same holds true for specialty lists, such as magazine subscriber lists. Sure, the readers of *Golf Digest* or

*Modern Maturity* may seem like good targets, and they may well be. But what about all those potential clients who don't read those particular magazines? Age combined with either income, home value, or investable assets should be sufficient filters for all but the most specialized campaigns.

It is, of course, critical to use a list that is accurate. The major list companies all update their lists regularly. Despite today's sophisticated address correction software, there is no such thing as a perfect mailing list. Literally tens of thousands of people move every day. People change their names. People die. It is impossible to keep up. Most major list providers maintain a 95% accuracy level, with some approaching 99%.

Your offer is also critically important to the success of your mail piece. For any direct mail piece to be effective, it must contain a well-defined offer and call to action. The specifics will vary depending on the focus of your mail piece and what you want it to accomplish. Are you looking to beef up your overall prospect database? Or perhaps your goal is to sell a specific annuity product strictly to high income Baby Boomers. You must first consider the type of response you want from your prospect. We're not talking about the number of responses, but *how* the prospects respond to you – and for what reason. Let's look at a couple of examples.

Say you send a letter of introduction to a targeted group of prospects. You list your accomplishments, credentials, etc. and then offer them a free 'financial check-up' if they call your office and schedule an appointment before the end of the month. You've offered them something of value, (financial check-up), and given them a specific call to action, (call your office before the end of the month). The people who respond to this offer are likely to be very good prospects. They are people in your age and income target who are willing to come down to your office and discuss their personal finances with you. Even though the quality of responses is high, chances are that the *quantity* of responses to a mailing like that would be fairly low. And, that may not matter. The mailing's response rate is not nearly as important as the value of the clients it ultimately produces.

Now consider another example. This time, you send the same targeted audience a mailer offering a free report on "10 Ways to Reduce Taxes". They can call, send back a business reply card, or e-mail their request to you. You again have offered something of value, (free report), and a specific call to action, (call, write or e-mail).

This second mailer will get a decidedly higher number of re-sponses than the first mailer because the prospects perceive their risk in responding to be much lower. Getting a free report requires a lot less commitment than a face to face meeting in your office. These prospects will take a little more work to convert to clients, but eventually, you should end up with more clients than you got from the first mailing.

Financial Advisors are faced with a great challenge when it comes to marketing. Because you are dealing with people's money – in many cases, their life savings – it is absolutely essential to estab-lish credibility and build trust. That isn't easy to accomplish with a single letter or postcard. Very few people are going to respond directly to a postcard that simply offers an annuity. Many advi-sors find a successful strategy is to make an initial low risk offer to the prospect, and then using subsequent contacts to move the relationship to the point of a meeting – and ultimately a sale.

Using the report mailing as an example; you could respond to the prospects who request a report by including a letter from you listing your credentials and a certificate for a free consultation. Why is that different from the first mailing? Now you have gained credibility by fulfilling your promise to send them something, and they have read your well written report addressing their financial concerns. You have established yourself with them and started a dialogue. Now, any future contact you initiate will not seem intrusive.

As you will see in the upcoming section, the same concept makes seminars an extremely effective marketing tool. The risk of attending is perceived as being fairly low, because the prospects aren't coming to an office. (The free meal doesn't hurt either.) You then get nearly an hour of their undivided attention to establish credibility and build trust.

Now that you have selected your list and have crafted an offer and call to action, the next step is to determine what kind of mail piece to use. Discuss your offer with your direct mail company and ask them what has been effective for other advisors with similar campaign goals. This is not to suggest you should do exactly the same thing as someone else. You are looking for a concept and package that you can make your own. There are several different standard mailing pieces to consider. Which one you choose will depend greatly on what you want to accomplish with your mailing.

The postcard is one of the most versatile and frequently utilized mail pieces. Whether you choose a smaller card, (4 x 6 inches, which mails at a First Class postage rate, but costs less than a full sized letter), or an "over-sized" postcard, (usually 6 x 9 inches and mails at the cheaper Standard Rate), depends on several factors. The smaller postcards do not have much room for copy, so the offer has to be brief and to the point. They are best used after you have established a relationship with a prospect rather than for an initial contact. Many advisors employ postcards as a follow up tool. Oversized postcards have more space, therefore more flexibility. You will often see one side of these larger cards devoted entirely to an eye-catching graphic or headline, with the copy on the flip side. One big advantage postcards have is that you don't have to open them. It is almost impossible not to at least glance at a postcard when you receive one in the mail. Your copy and graphics must capture the recipient's attention in that split second they look at it while shuffling through the mail. A well designed postcard will do just that.

Self-mailers possess the same attention-getting qualities as postcards, and offer even more flexibility -- both in size and function. They can range from a simple trifold corporate brochure to elaborate multi–panel masterpieces. Self-mailers are used when you need more space to tell your story. When folded to mailing size, one side is usually reserved for a headline or teaser copy, with the other side used for addressing the piece. It is also a good idea to include a tear off response card when using a self-mailer. As a general rule, you should always give your prospects several different ways to respond to your offer. The method they choose for responding can also give you an indication of their interest level. People who use reply cards may be interested in more information, whereas someone who calls or sends an e-mail could be a "hotter" prospect.

There are some experts who will tell you that using an envelope will hurt your response. That is not entirely true. The success of an envelope based mailing depends entirely on the presentation. It is true that a simple envelope adorned with a bulk mail indicia and an address label screams "junk mail". It is an easy decision for someone, who gets a package like that in the mail, not to open it. Your challenge is to make it a difficult decision. To do that, the envelope either has to look like personal correspondence, a government notice, a check - anything that says "you better open me." Today's technology allows your direct mail company to directly address your envelope with a handwritten font, create personalized letters, and even personalized Post-it notes. Spending a few extra dollars on personalization and live postage stamps will do wonders for your response. Your direct mail company will offer suggestions and let you know what has been successful for them.

Now that you have put the list, offer, call to action and package together, do you send your mailing using First Class postage or Standard Class, (better know as Bulk Rate)? There are very few instances, other than noted above, where you should use First Class. The main reason is the cost difference. First Class runs an average of 10¢ more than Bulk. That can add up in a hurry on larger mailings. The only exception would be promoting a dated event, like a seminar – especially if you are behind schedule. First Class mail gets delivered in 1-2 days locally, whereas Bulk mail is less predictable and can take much longer. Your direct mail company is your best source of advice. They don't profit from the postage charges, so there is no conflict of interest in recommending the right choice for your particular mailing project. They can also offer alternatives, such as drop shipping, to expedite your delivery while still keeping your costs down.

After you actually execute your mailing, you need to analyze the results. Direct mail is a uniquely measurable medium; and you should take full advantage of the opportunity to examine your responses. What kind of information can you get? The first thing to look at is where your responses came from. Which zips codes pulled the best ratio of response? Your mailing company can tell you how many pieces went to each zip. You may be able to isolate pockets of strength and utilize that knowledge in future mailings. You can do the same with age group – even gender. If you mailed to a 55+ age group, but the bulk of your responses came from 60-65 year olds, perhaps you should target your next mailing more specifically.

What you don't want to do is make any snap judgments after one mailing – especially if your mailing didn't do as well as you might have expected. Speaking of expectations, what is considered a good response?

The industry 'standard' you most often hear is 1%. This is some-what misleading, because there are so many variations between mail pieces, offers, and response methods. The numbers will also vary from mailing to mailing. To measure the success of a mailing, you need to know the following:

- Your mailing costs (design, printing, list, postage – everything)
- How much an average client is worth to you , in dollar figures
- The percentage of inquiries you can turn into appointments
- Your closing ratio

For example, let's say you send out 10,000 mail pieces, and your total cost to execute the mailing is $5,000. If you get a 1/2%

response, that's 50 people. If you can turn 20% of those into office appointments, that gives you 10. At a closing ratio of 50%, you will end up with 5 new clients. Using a lifetime value of $2,500 per client, your $5,000 investment has returned $12,500 worth of revenue – an impressive 150% ROI.

Even though the mailing was clearly profitable, you may be disappointed with your 1/2% response rate if you went in with the preconceived notion that anything less than 1% is considered a failure. *The bottom line is results, not an arbitrary percentage.* You have to look at your own costs, closing ratios and the value of an average client. Your closing ratio may be lower than 50%, or your average client may be worth much more than $2,500. Plug your own (honest) numbers into the formula and see if it makes sense for you. If you are like most advisors, netting just one or two clients from a mailing will cover your costs. The rest is icing on the cake.

That is the beauty of direct mail as it applies to financial marketers. Because each client you gain is typically worth thousands of dollars to you over time, you don't need to get a huge response to make direct mail a very effective -- and lucrative -- prospecting tool.

Even if you are satisfied with the results of your campaign, you should always strive to do better. Could you have gotten a better response? Better *qualified* responses? The only way to find out is to keep mailing – and testing. Change one aspect of your package and see if you get a better response. In some cases "better" may actually mean less total responses, but more clients – or more revenue.

*What* you change will depend on where you think you need improvement. For instance, if your mailing generated a lot of leads, but the prospects you actually sat down with didn't have the assets you were hoping for; try raising your income filter. Or perhaps you could use a different filter such as home value. If the respondents seemed qualified, but the number of responses was on the low side, try altering the offer slightly, or maybe use a different headline. A word of caution: you can't test more than one variable on the same mailing piece, or you will have no idea which variable caused the change in response.

One good testing method is called an "A/B Split". Basically, you divide your mailing list into two equal parts. Part A will get one version of the mailing, and part B will get the other. You could, for example, send out postcards and test different headlines to see which gets the best response. Or, you could try mailing a postcard to part A and a personalized letter to part B. In this case the offer would be the same, but the package is different. If you can pull as many responses from a postcard as you can from a much more expensive letter; you just saved yourself a bunch of money. On the other hand, you may find that the additional cost of the letter package is more than justified by the number (or quality) of prospects it produces.

After testing different packages, you will eventually come up with the most effective combination of mailing list, offer, call to action, and presentation. This becomes your "control" package; the one by which you measure all of your subsequent efforts. As long as there aren't any notable changes to the market, you should be able to mail your control package with confidence that it will generate the same results time after time.

No matter how good your mailing results are, there will still be a significant number of prospects who don't immediately become clients. Let's take another look at the numbers from our previous example. The 10,000 piece mailing costs $5,000. A 1/2% response yielded 50 prospects. Out of the 10 people who made appointments, 5 eventually became clients. Most advisors would look at those numbers and be pleased. After all, those 5 clients are very likely to generate much more income than the $5,000 spent to acquire them. But most advisors aren't top producers. A top producer would look at those numbers and see the potential of the remaining 45 prospects who didn't become clients.

Think about it. You have identified 45 people who fit your client profile and have taken the time to express an interest in your services. Shouldn't you market to them some more? Granted, some of these people will never become your clients for one reason or another. But based on your CPR, you have already invested $100 each on these prospects. Doesn't it make sense to invest a few more dollars a month to convert them into clients? Top producers certainly think so.

The best way to work with these prospects is a technique known as *Drip Marketing*. You should start by building a database of prospects from mailings, referrals, seminars – anyone who has shown interest but hasn't become a client. Make note of the date they were added to list. Then, mail them something every month. It doesn't have to be an elaborate mail piece. Any useful financial information is fine. Some advisors send a copy of a magazine article with a Post-it note attached. Newsletters work extremely well. In fact, Acquire Direct Marketing has created a turn key drip marketing newsletter that advisors can personalize with their own contact information.

This is passive marketing. Resist the temptation to "touch base" with repeated phone calls. You just want to keep your name in front of these prospects. Let your drip marketing material do its work. Every time a prospect receives something from you, it further establishes your credibility and shows that you have a genuine interest. Prospects who don't respond to a drip marketing piece within 6 months should be removed from the list.

Drip marketing is deceptively simple, yet remarkably effective. It should become a logical extension of any lead generation marketing you do. Think of it as lead *cultivation*. Not every piece of fruit ripens at the same time; and some hang lower on the tree than others. Prospects are the same way. Some take a little extra time and effort, but the rewards are well worth it.

# Xponent Marketing™

At this point, we have covered enough topics to address our marketing philosophy, which we refer to as *Xponent Marketing™*.

Xponent Marketing™ is different from traditional marketing. The main distinction is that traditional marketing focuses on locating people who are ready to buy immediately. The problem is that this is a relatively small number of people. Obviously, the pool of people who may not buy today, but who are going to eventually buy, is many, many times larger. Xponent Marketing™ focuses on this larger group. Traditional marketing is like fishing with a hook and line. Xponent Marketing™ is like fishing with a net.

The first step to understanding the concept of Xponent Marketing™ is to analyze the Buying Continuum:

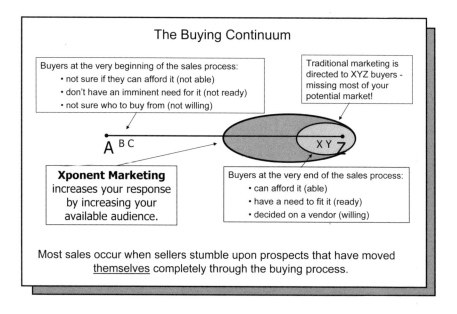

Xponent Marketing™ helps you look at all sales prospects between two points on the buying continuum, one to the left (A) and one to the right (Z).

The A prospects are at the very beginning of the buying continuum. They aren't ready to make a purchase or don't feel the need to do so any time soon. They may be qualified; they just aren't ready yet.

The Z prospects are at the other end of the sales process. Either through desire or necessity; they are ready to buy. Traditional marketing focuses on the X, Y and Z end of the scale. Using our example from the previous chapter, these are the prospects who will respond immediately to the mailing that offered a free consultation for anyone who makes an appointment before the end of the month. You may be asking, "What's wrong with prospects that are ready to buy?" Nothing, of course. But, the problem you face as a financial advisor is there just aren't that many people who are ready to become clients immediately. If you were selling pizzas, you would have a much larger percentage of prospects at that end of the buying continuum.

Xponent Marketing™ focuses on those prospects at the midpoint on the continuum all the way over to X. This does not mean you are eliminating those potential buyers at X, Y, and Z, but you are going to structure a marketing offer that will also appeal to those people who are not quite ready yet. If your mailing list is targeted properly, everyone who receives your offer will be qualified to work with you. What we are talking about here is their *readiness* to buy – and their *willingness* to buy from you.

Take a look at the next graphic:

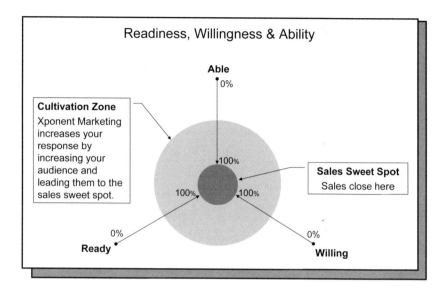

There are three conditions to every sale

1. You can never have a sale unless your prospect is **ready** to buy. Remember that some sales are situational, which means the buyer has no choice but to act. Other sales are discretionary, but the buyer is still determined he must have your product or service.

2. Prospects must be **able** to buy. Most people won't seriously consider buying until they know they have the ability. Sometimes a transaction just isn't possible under any circumstances. Targeting your prospects correctly should eliminate most prospects that are unable to work with you in some capacity.

3. The prospect has to be **willing** to buy from **you**. If you are utilizing a carefully developed direct mail campaign, your prospects should be age qualified – giving you a prospect

> that is **Ready** for your services and they should be income or asset qualified – which gives them the **Ability** to use your services. Now you just need to make them **Willing** to hire you!

The key concept is to create an offer that will draw responses from a wider section of the buying continuum. Remember the "free report" offer from the previous chapter? This is an example of Xponent Marketing™ in action. Many more people will respond to an offer for a free report than one that requires them to immediately call your office to make an appointment. As a result, you have a much larger pool of prospects to work with. Take a look at the following chart to see how the perceived risk of an offer affects the response:

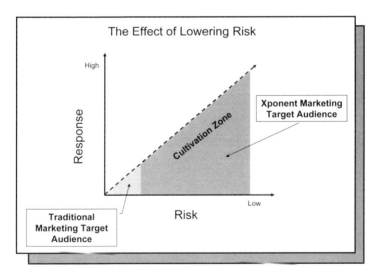

It makes perfect sense -- the lower the risk, the higher the response. Going back to our free report example; the prospects that were already close to making a buying decision will be the ones who take immediate advantage of the certificate for a free consultation you sent them along with their report, and quickly make appointments. You are still getting the prime X, Y and Z prospects. However, by using a low risk offer, you are also getting a large number of qualified prospects -- prospects that you would have missed with a higher risk offer -- who may not be quite willing to buy yet.

What do you do with the rest of the prospects that aren't ready to buy? You teach them to buy from you. This is the real meat of Xponent Marketing™. You move them along the buying continuum until they are willing to buy from you. You do this by educating them. How do you educate them? You educate them by continuing to market to them. This is where the drip marketing system we touched on in the last chapter really comes into play.

You can send them newsletters, financial articles, white papers – anything that will demonstrate your knowledge, build your credibility, and keep your name in front of them. Something in one of the articles may catch their eye or hit a hot button. If nothing else, you are establishing yourself as the benchmark financial advisor in the area by which they judge your competitors. It may take some prospects quite some time to move through the process, but each contact you make with them should nudge them closer to the "Z" end of the continuum. When they finally reach that point, your chances of being the advisor they are willing to buy from are exponentially increased because of your drip marketing efforts. Over a period of time you become their natural choice.

The next section of the Marketing for Millions is devoted to seminar marketing, which is the epitome of Xponent Marketing™. You make a relatively low risk offer, (free meal at a nice venue), to a qualified target, (based on your mailing list). After the seminar, a certain percentage of attendees will immediately make appointments, (prospects at the X, Y and Z end of the buying continuum), while others will need to be educated further before they become clients, (through drip marketing).

The idea of Xponent Marketing™ is the single most important concept in this book. The subject probably deserves an entire book of its own  If nothing else, perhaps this brief outline will get you thinking about marketing in a different way.

# Seminar
# Marketing

# Why Conduct A Seminar?

Every financial professional knows that seminars are the fastest way to build new business. It really is that simple. Seminars work better than any other marketing tool in the financial services industry.

There is simply no way to get in front of more qualified prospects than to conduct a financial seminar. There is no quicker way to make a personal connection with future clients than to speak to them directly at your own event. With the virtual demise of telemarketing, there is no better way to set appointments with prospects other than securing a commitment from them at your event.

Seminars offer another unique advantage. That is anonymity. While it may be difficult to get a prospect to come in for a first appointment even if he or she comes from a referral, most people will attend a seminar. A seminar allows prospective clients to sit back and size you up from afar. In other words, it is a method of marketing that puts very little pressure on those being marketed. It also allows you to put your best foot forward under circumstances that are almost completely under your control.

So why isn't every financial advisor using seminar marketing? Most don't know how to put together a successful seminar. Some are afraid of public speaking. Some are wary of the financial commitment. And, many simply don't have the drive to market aggressively.

Seminar marketing means reaching out to thousands of prospects, speaking to hundreds of potential clients and doing business with more new customers in one year than some advisors handle in an entire career. In fact, one of the major challenges you will face will be how to schedule seminars so the follow up appointments they generate don't overwhelm you and your staff.

Of course, financial seminars don't work for everyone. There are many stories of advisors who have tried to put on a seminar and failed. Usually the advisors who fail haven't taken the time to prepare properly or they have tried to cut corners with cheap invitations or postcards that sell the restaurant instead of the seminar content.

Success is all about preparation, execution and follow-through. It's all about working with the right suppliers, audience-friendly restaurants, and well trained in-house staff. Seminars are a serious investment. Some advisors are skeptical of seminars because they worry that they are feeding people whose only intention is to come and eat. There is no denying that. But it is simply part of the price of doing business. You can control this to some extent by limiting the number of guests each attendee is allowed to bring, putting minimum age restrictions on all attendees, and making sure that everyone who has attended is deleted from your seminar prospect list for one year. Of course, the real pros even motivate the eaters into making appointments through a compelling presentation. As a sophisticated marketing tool, seminars require as much attention to detail as any financial instrument in your professional arsenal.

The intent of the following chapters is to help you optimize your seminar marketing dollar and to help you achieve the maximum return on your investment. Most advisors who conduct seminars book appointments with 25% to 30% of the attendees or "buying units", (this term counts couples as one unit). However, if you follow the guidelines in this book, you should expect to see at least 50% of your prospects request an appointment. In fact, there have been seminars given in which every single buying unit booked an appointment to meet with the advisor!

A really good seminar marketing system will enable you to:
- Attract the most qualified prospects to your seminar
- Demonstrate your financial expertise to new prospects
- Build trust and rapport with your audience
- Improve the efficiency and effectiveness of your marketing effort
- Increase your professional satisfaction by helping you achieve your marketing objectives

Get ready to succeed beyond your greatest expectations. Seminars hold the key for financial professionals who take the time and make the effort to get the marketing right.

# Creating Compelling Presentations

Every successful seminar marketer begins by creating a compelling presentation. The importance of the word "compelling" cannot be overstated because the points you make in your presentation will probably become the bullet points you use for your invitations and other seminar promotional materials. But before you begin work on your presentation, there are a few decisions you will need to make.

The first of these decisions is whether to go through the challenge of creating your own presentation or purchase a ready made presentation. There are, of course, pros and cons to each method.

A ready-made presentation carries with it an enormous benefit if compliance is an issue, because it has been reviewed by the NASD. You should definitely inquire about the status of any presentation before you make a purchase. If it has been officially reviewed by the NASD, it most likely means few problems with your broker dealer. These presentations are usually more graphically sophisticated, because the companies that specialize in them sell them in large numbers and can afford the best graphic designers.

On the negative side, you run the very real risk that another advisor in your area is using the exact same presentation, unless you have been guaranteed a specific territory. Often, ready-made presentations are quite generic and institutional in content and appearance. They may be based on a single topic, and they probably don't contain the exact mix of strategies and products that you would prefer.

However, you may be able to customize a ready-made presentation. In fact, many advisors wind up doing exactly that. The problem is that they often wind up with a seminar that has visual components which don't match and poor transitions between topics; resulting in a presentation that doesn't have a logical flow. It is more difficult to customize a ready-made PowerPoint® than one would imagine, and any changes you make will have to be reviewed by your compliance department.

Another option is to hire a company that specializes in custom financial PowerPoints®. You create your own presentation and leave it to the experts to design the graphics. If you do decide to do it yourself, this chapter contains some tips on how to follow the process.

This chapter has been written under the assumption that you are going to use PowerPoint® in your presentation. There are advisors who say that they find PowerPoint® bothersome and distracting. They would prefer to just get up in front of an audience and talk, because all eyes are always on them instead of the screen. While this may be easier for you, it does not make things easier for your audience. Quite simply, people process information differently. Some people learn better visually, and some people learn better by what they hear. If you take away the visual component, you may be reducing some attendees' comprehension by half. This becomes even more important if you are marketing to retirees, many of whom have some degree of hearing loss.

Frequently during your presentation, you may need to illustrate a financial concept by using numbers. In this case there is nothing wrong with pulling out a white board, but it is more effectively used as an addition to a PowerPoint® rather than as a replacement. Just make sure when you do so that your writing is legible from the seats at the very back of the room.

There is another very good reason for giving your presentation with a PowerPoint®. It is currently the gold standard. If you do anything less, you risk appearing less professional. On the other hand, don't get carried away by the use of technology. Some PowerPoint® presentations now include video portions as well. These are much more susceptible to technical problems.

Success in creating a seminar presentation begins with your initiative and insight. No one knows your local market better than you do. Visualizing a successful seminar begins with defining your ideal prospect. Who are the people in your region you want to work with or have the most investable assets? You should know this if you have done your targeting studies.

The most important attribute of a good financial seminar is relevance. You will capture and hold your attendees' attention if you speak directly to their needs in every aspect of your seminar campaign. By profiling your potential client base, you can discover the appropriate financial products to offer your target market. Of course, you should never mention products directly. Refer to them as strategies instead. Just remember to keep the discussion of your favorite product to no more than 25% of your presentation.

Also be aware, discussing topics that are not relevant to a majority of your audience can cause them to tune out quickly. For example, if you are presenting to prospects with moderate to low net worth, you will only alienate your target market by promoting strategies to avoid inheritance taxes. Their lack of interest will be obvious just by their body language.

Long term care insurance may hold little appeal to the very wealthy. They may self-insure or have other avenues for long term care coverage. On the other hand, the wealthy will have a strong interest in tax avoidance strategies, and the very wealthy in inheritance tax strategies. Municipal bonds, dividend producing instruments, some forms of trusts, and annuities could be highly attractive to that target market. As you continue to give your seminars, you will learn what to highlight and what to eliminate.

Even geographic areas that are relatively low income will provide opportunities among prospects who have gathered a reasonable pool of equity. While CRTs and long term care may be out of the question, other vehicles that provide secure income during retirement and shelter from taxes on social security payments always create audience interest. Middle class investors often assume they are free from death taxes. Your seminar can remind them that even they will face taxes at death on their IRAs unless they take advantage of your expertise with the Stretch IRA. You might also consider promoting the huge savings that trusts may provide. Even in the lower income neighborhoods, there are investment instruments, such as reverse mortgages, that can become powerful tools in your seminar marketing arsenal.

The important thing to remember is to keep revising the components of your PowerPoint® presentation until you feel you have the best mix of products and strategies. This is easily gauged by the number of appointments you set -- if everything else is in order. Don't be fooled into thinking you have constructed the perfect presentation by the compliments you receive. People tend to be more positive than they truly feel on seminar evaluation sheets. Nothing counts but numbers. If you receive requests for appointments from fewer than 30% of the buying units in the audience, you need to go back to the drawing board.

The most common mistake advisors make is trying to impress their audience by giving them every single detail. This results in a seminar that is overly complicated and way too long. You should aim for a completion time of about 50 minutes with a five minute break at the point right before you show the audience any complex strategies or calculations. This allows the audience time to give their brains a rest before you demand their intense concentration. As a matter of fact, it is important to allow "brain catch up" times throughout your presentation. There will be more advice on how to do this in the chapter on giving your presentation.

As many authorities on public speaking have said before, the pattern for optimum audience comprehension is the following: "Tell people what you are going to tell them. Then tell them. Then tell them what you have told them." In other words, outline your topics and objectives, give your talk, and then summarize what you have said in a way the audience is going to remember.

Begin by defining a broad based hot button that is likely to interest everyone. Let them know how important it is and why they should care about it. One way to do this is to add a special touch to the typical pattern for speechmaking. Give your audience a "promise of performance" at the outset. Tell them that you will provide at least one tip that they will be able to put to work immediately to improve their finances. Providing such a tip should not be a challenge for any financial professional. At the end of the talk, ask the audience if you kept your promise of performance. Did you provide them with at least one tip that will make a difference in their financial lives? Inevitably many will answer "yes".

Features of a financial product or strategy are not effective motivators for seminar audiences. Few people will have any interest in the mechanics of important financial instruments like trusts. A straight educational lecture will not hold their attention.

But speak to your audience about profit and loss, and you will have their interest. Personally involve them by showing people important mistakes they may be making with their financial strategies. Make it plain how much these mistakes may cost them or their heirs. Underline the fact that such losses are unnecessary.

Show the benefits to your audience by discussing solutions; and make it plain how these solutions work. Quantify how much your audience might stand to gain by putting their mistakes behind them and employing your solutions.

Another part of this approach which helps audiences remember is a "personal touch". Usually a personal touch involves telling the story of a client who was helped by using a particular strategy you employed. Provide as much personal detail as possible without using the client's real name. Describe his or her predicament and the effect it had on their lives. Describe the solution and how it materially changed their lives for the better.

Specific detail is the key to this strategy. It's not enough to say that your sample client was experiencing hardship. Provide detail such as: "She hadn't been able to afford a visit to see her grandchildren for five years." Detail exactly how the solution changed that problem. For instance: "She saved $1,200 in Social Security tax right away, and the first thing she did was buy a ticket to California to see her grandchildren."

Sure that may sound overly sentimental. You will probably choose entirely different stories from your own client base. The important thing is to illustrate your financial talk with human specifics. You will make a much greater impact during your speech. And, when you see seminar prospects in an appointment, they may not remember tax and investment strategies clearly, but they will remember your stories. They won't recall the specifics of using annuities to avoid taxes, but they will remember to ask you about the strategy that helped your client visit her grandchildren by reducing social security tax.

So far this discussion has been all about what you say, but not about what your audience sees on the PowerPoint®. "See" is the operative word because every component should be visible from the most distant seat in the house. The rule of thumb in creating PowerPoint® presentations is no more than six bullet points per slide, and no more than six words per bullet point. However, if you can find strong supporting visuals, you may wish to use fewer. Also, make sure your charts and graphs are legible. Your best source for these is Ibbotson, or materials from your broker dealer. Just make sure the information is no more than one year old.

No matter what the asset level of your audience is, you want a professional looking presentation. This means avoiding clip art and cartoons. Instead you can find appropriate high quality photos on *Comstock.com* or the less expensive *Photospin*. You will also make your PowerPoint® more cohesive if you use the same background color throughout. However, if you do wish to emphasize a shift in your presentation, then by all means change your background color to signal a new topic.

The other key is pacing. The general rule is to use one slide every three minutes. But unless bullet points are animated to come up individually, that can be an awfully long time. If you vary the pacing somewhere between 30 seconds and three minutes, your presentation will be far more interesting.

The interaction between you and the PowerPoint® is also extremely important. Except in certain circumstances which will be addressed later, you never want to turn your back to the audience and read verbatim. The PowerPoint® is there to enhance what you say. This brings up another point. It is essential that you practice giving your seminar without the aid of your PowerPoint® because at some time or other, you are going to experience a technical failure. You must be able to continue your presentation without missing a beat, and your audience will consider you to be a true pro.

# Preparing Your Materials

Assemble your seminar handout packets well in advance at your office. These require considerable preparation. An attractive presentation folder along with a professional looking brochure will significantly enhance your image. Here are some elements you should consider when putting together your handout package:

- The folder should be printed with your company name and logo
- Include biographies of financial advisors, professional associates and company staff printed on high quality paper
- Include your business card, professionally printed with your logo plainly visible
- Include articles written by or about you. If you have none, insert article reprints on seminar-related topics. If you do insert outside articles, use no more than three and make sure they are not more than one year old
- Insert your company brochure and a brochure from your broker dealer
- Include a financial planning guide and an appointment/evaluation card
- Provide note paper and matching pens

Here's an important touch that few seminar marketers bother with, (which is all the more reason you should). In addition to providing nametags for your guests, also produce a personalized welcome letter. Use the list of seminar attendees in your computer and mail merge their names with your welcome letter. This technique always makes a strong first impression. But remember this extremely important point: *nothing will ruin that good first impression more quickly than spelling someone's name wrong.* If you are going to use personalized letters, double check everything to make sure there are no errors.

At your sign in table, lay out your folders with the printed matching nametags clipped to the top. As your attendees and their guests arrive, your staff will present them with their personalized materials and sign them in on your tracking chart. Remember to always have a few extra generic folders on hand. Sometimes a husband and wife will each want their own folder, and you should oblige them.

Advisors often say that clients sometimes keep their printed materials for as much as a year before setting a first appointment. Many prospects bring the advisor's full complement of printed matter back at appointment time, carefully saved and mixed in with financial statements and other documents. Clearly, any marketing piece which enters a client's home should be perceived as something worth holding on to. It will surely be seen as a reflection of the advisor's own level of professionalism and worth. It must give the unmistakable impression that it is an object of value.

In order to create top quality materials with a cohesive look, you will need to go through a process that requires a bit of graphic and verbal artistry. It is important to find a reasonable balance between quality and cost. That means, formulate your printing budget to include the creation of several marketing and image-building pieces. No single piece can address all of your marketing needs. Beware of any consultant who tells you that one expensive piece alone will do the whole job.

The function of any printed material leaving your seminar or office is to build positive perceptions of you and your practice among potential clients. That's why the layout and design must meet or exceed the level of quality that your prospects are accustomed to in materials they receive from other financial companies -- even national corporations. Style, color palettes and printing fonts should match throughout your entire range of printed materials. Text should be brief and to the point -- but never simplistic or patronizing. Professional photography is a must. Be prepared to invest in the services of a graphic designer, copywriter, and photographer.

This is not a suggestion to run out and spend a fortune on printed matter. Unfortunately, there are many advisors who have been persuaded to spend more than $10,000 on a *single brochure* by a marketing company that specializes in branding financial professionals individually. If this sounds a bit extravagant, you are absolutely correct. You can put together a beautiful package without spending a fortune. But, the trick is to know the difference between being frugal – and downright cheap.

When you work with a copywriter and graphic designer to compose brochures, folders, business cards, letterhead and so forth, you first need to determine the exact specifications you want to use. These would include, paper size, weight and quality, ink colors, and any special finishing, (die cutting, foil stamping, etc). This will assure you get the look you want from your printer.

Make sure when you design your pocket folder that you do not print your address or phone number on the piece itself. Rather, have business card slits added so your card fits neatly into the pocket. It's more likely that your address will change before your logo does. The more information you include on your folders, the more likely something will change; and you'll end up tossing them in the dumpster.

Your logo is vitally important. Consumers respond to and remember visuals. That's why so many companies focus on the creation of a logo as the first step in creating their image.

A logo should evoke a response consistent with the image an advisor wishes to create. Plan on using a graphic artist who is experienced in logo design. The charge may be as much as $125 an hour to create three or four designs to choose from. The process will depend on your ability to articulate your own concepts and on the artist's vision. Custom logo design can easily cost more than a thousand dollars. Regardless, this is a job for a competent graphic artist. Do not attempt to design your own logo. It will be printed on all your material and give a quality national look to your identity.

A basic question you should ask yourself first is: "How do you wish your firm to be perceived, as traditional or cutting edge?" Often the answer is "both". But look a little deeper. Look at your client profile, your office, and consider your own personal style. When you conduct a detailed examination, you will often see a proclivity in one direction or another. Consistency of image is crucial, and it is an essential starting point to define the true nature of an advisor's own image and target clientele. Keep in mind that a logo is not just composed of a pictorial representation. It is also made up of words requiring decisions about fonts, word placement and proportion.

Now that you have your logo and your color scheme, you are ready to create the cover for your handout. This is your presentation folder. Ask your printer, to give you actual samples -- or at least a swatch book -- of their paper stock. There are many paper manufacturers that offer letterhead, business card and envelope stock that will match or complement your folder. Beckett Cambric, Classic Crest, and Strathmore are a few examples.

If you do everything correctly, you will create a product that will be the basis for seminar presentation folders, logos, brochures and stationery which harmonize with the pieces provided by your broker dealer.

There are a few final words of caution. Although it adds to the time and the price, always request proofs and inspect them very carefully. Then, proof the corrected proof! If you do not sign off on a final proof and an error is found after the piece is printed, you will have no recourse except to re-print the job at your expense. Signing a proof releases the printer from all responsibility in regards to typos, positioning, etc. Also, when ordering your printed material, be aware that many printers allow for a quantity variation of plus or minus 10%. This means you should not estimate your number in a way that could produce a shortfall. If there is any question, ask your printer about it up front.

One can't help being surprised by the poor standard of printed materials distributed by many financial advisors; even some "elite" practices who aim at capturing high net worth clients. Good quality paper stock and printing, professional graphic design, and well-written copy are essential. After all, your printed materials are the only tangible item that potential clients take home with them after your seminar.

Image-making of this sort may not automatically draw clients, but it still serves an important purpose. Your printed material will make a lasting impression with your prospective clients. It is up to you to make sure that impression is a good one.

# Establishing A Timeline

## Ten Weeks In Advance

1. Create your presentation, taking care to establish pertinent topics that will later become bullet points for your invitations.

2. Do a demographic analysis to determine your target audience and set an approximate budget.

3. Survey possible venues and speak to the restaurant or hotel food and beverage or special events manager in person. Take along the checklist provided in this book, (see appendix), and see if you can bargain with the promise of future events -- if all goes well.

4. If you do not already have a logo and high quality brochure, as well as a professionally written biography, hire a copywriter and a graphic artist. Be sure to request samples of their work first.

5. Hire a seminar coordinator and extra assistant. Have a backup assistant in case of emergencies or extra large crowds which will require two people at the sign in desk.

6. If you do not have them already, start pricing the cost of a large screen, sound system and projector. If you decide to rent them, find out what they will cost if provided by the venue. You will also greatly benefit by using a podium.

## Eight Weeks in Advance

1. Submit your PowerPoint® and script along with your brochure and any other newly written materials to your compliance department as required.

2. Contact seminar marketing companies, ask for sample invitations, mailing list counts and pricing.

3. Choose a printer to produce your presentation folders. Begin the process of having them print your folders. Expect to exchange proofs several times.

4. Make the final selection for your venues. Draw up a written contract that will include the following: seminar dates, a pricing guarantee, choice of meals, beverages, snacks for the tables and during the break, equipment rental if necessary, the number of hours in advance you can access the room to begin your own setup, the number of days in advance they will require an exact meal count, penalties for under or overestimating, any free extras such as valet parking or room decorations you have managed to negotiate, and exact copies of room layout for various numbers of attendees, (this should also show the position of the projector table, the break table, and the sign in table). Keep a copy of the entire contract to bring with you the day of the event.

5. Choose your seminar reservation service and give them a script to follow. Make sure you are assigned a toll-free number, which your seminar marketing company will need for your invitations.

6. Send off all copies of material to be printed to the printing company or companies you have chosen. Don't forget extra stationary with your new graphic design and logo.

7. Begin practicing your presentation daily. Look for an opportunity to give your presentation to a live audience, such as a public service club, before you deliver it at a seminar you have paid for.

## *Seven Weeks in Advance*

1. Select a competent seminar marketing company. A good company will recommend an invitation style and help you structure a message that will generate maximum results.

2. Send a copy of your invitation to compliance at your broker dealer if required. Make sure you don't sign-off on the proof until you have approval from compliance.

3. Create signage for your event.

## Six Weeks in Advance

1. Purchase all necessary equipment. Include extra extension cords and power strips, batteries, an extra projector bulb, gaffer tape, and scissors. Keep these small items packed in a permanent kit you take to every seminar.

2. Inform your seminar marketing company that your invitations have passed compliance and let them know they have your permission to mail your invite on the day you jointly agree is appropriate.

3. Create your seminar appointment cards and assemble all materials that go into your handout, including special articles.

4. Purchase high quality printable name tags. You will also need pens that coordinate with your folder color. You can use your stationery for notes instead of paying extra for imprinted pads.

5. Compose your own seminar reservation letters, seminar welcome letters, post-seminar thank you letters and first appointment follow up letters, or use the samples provided in this book, (see appendix).

## Four Weeks In Advance

1. You should have received all printed copies of your presentation folders, brochures and stationery.

2. Prepare and print maps to the seminar venue and to your office.

3. Learn to give your presentation without using the PowerPoint®. This will prepare you if you ever have to deal with equipment failure.

4. Choose the person who is going to introduce you at the seminar. Then write the introduction and have the chosen person memorize it and practice it so it can be delivered naturally, with conviction.

5. Activate your RSVP phone line.

## *Two Weeks In Advance*

1. Meet with the staff to finalize all seminar duties and confirm the attendance of your extra assistant.

2. Select your music.

3. Invitations should have already been sent out, so be prepared to handle the RSVPs. Ask that your seminar reservation service send you an Excel® spreadsheet on a daily basis with the names of all attendees and their guests in alphabetical order. This will save time at check-in. If the service gives you a link to a web portal to access your respondents, check it several times a day.

4. Have your seminar coordinator or reservation service reconfirm all the attendees and their guests by telephone. Use these calls to fill out your tracking sheet, (you will find an example in the appendix of this book). As soon as you have spoken to the prospective attendees by phone, send out a seminar confirmation letter. Be sure to include a map to the venue and any parking instructions or special instructions for the handicapped.

## *One Week In Advance*

1. Organize handout packets. Don't forget to include the mail merge welcome letter and attach the printed matching nametags. Assume you will give out one packet per buying unit, but have a few extras for those who insist on having their own.

2. Test the projector, computer hookups and sound system. Make sure at least two people on your seminar staff know how to hook up all components.

3. Make a backup copy of your PowerPoint® presentation and your attendee list. The advisor and the seminar coordinator should each take copies of both items to the event.

## *Two Days before the Event*

1. Phone each attendee to reconfirm, then give your final count to the venue at the agreed upon time.
2. Reconfirm all contract details with the venue, particularly if your numbers require a choice of seating layouts.
3. Pack-up all your equipment, signage, and handouts.
4. Reconfirm timing and duties with your staff.

## *Day of the Event*

1. Speak to the RSVP service to make sure there were no last minute additions or cancellations. If so, let the venue know.
2. See the checklist in the appendix of this book for other items required on the day of the event.

# Selecting Your Location

You may hope that seminar attendees will show up merely for the pleasure of hearing you speak. Unfortunately, that's not entirely true. Even qualified prospects have become accustomed to being offered a meal with a financial seminar. Offering a good meal at an attractive location has become a part of the cost of doing business for seminar marketers.

If your market allows, you should select a venue within a 20 minute drive from your target mailing zone. Choose a restaurant with a strong reputation for high quality food and a comfortable atmosphere. Don't go overboard and don't try to get by on the cheap.

Holding a seminar at a coffee shop is not likely to attract anyone with a reasonable level of investable assets. Choosing a venue that is widely recognized for good food and a comfortable atmosphere will attract clients with higher net worth. Country clubs and private clubs can be intimidating to non-members, and experience shows that seminar prospects tend to avoid them. High-end hotels are a better draw, but depending on your market, they can be a bit pricey. The best draw is usually an established restaurant with a good reputation, or a brand new venue that people in your area are eager to try out.

Your seminar venue should have a senior-friendly atmosphere. One way to find an appropriate location for your prospects is to pick a place that is already popular with your target market, (in most cases, seniors). This is more difficult than it might seem. Many popular spots have no meeting rooms. Some are not willing to negotiate meal prices even if you offer them a great deal of business with a long term contract.

A few seminar consultants refer to the practice of staging financial seminars as a science. Nothing could be further from the truth. There are very few hard and fast rules about choosing a seminar venue because every region and every market is different. In Florida, for example, prospects are often attracted to larger resort hotels which have good parking facilities and a better than average reputation for food and service. But in many urban areas, hotels may not be your best choice because local prospects view the environment as geared to the transient business traveler.

Offer your invitees the option of more than one location per invitation. Keep careful records of the turnout at each location. If you get a significantly better response to one location than another, stay with what works. (Use the seminar tracking charts provided in the appendix).

If the differences are small, try offering multiple locations again on your next seminar invitation. It is possible that external factors may have driven down attendance at one location on a given day. It may perform well on another date.

If you have found more than one location that draws satisfactory crowds; congratulations! Use all that you have. Good locations are hard to find. Some prospects will prefer one over another due to the distance from their home or the atmosphere the venue provides. By offering more than one venue you will be casting a wider net. Your chances of attracting more qualified prospects will increase if your locations offer your guests a choice of delicious sounding entrees.

It is essential to visit your seminar locations in person and rate them according to a number of criteria that go well beyond the quality of the food. It's best to rely on a checklist of essentials (use the checklist in the appendix).

# Scheduling Your Event

Scheduling your seminar dates is the most difficult of all the variables you must deal with, because your schedule will never stay static. Local and world events and other outside factors are always at play. Add inclement weather and your own unforeseen conflicts and you can see that your schedule is always dynamic.

Assuming you have found your best mix of locations, you should set up a schedule of seminars for the next 12 months. While this schedule is not set in stone, it gives you the ability to approach your favorite venues with some degree of bargaining power.

The first decision you will need to make is whether you do indeed intend to give seminars all year long or just during certain times of the year. Many advisors make the mistake of discontinuing seminars over the summer because they feel it is just too difficult to get attendees. That's true, but only to a certain degree. In order to get the requisite attendance at summer events, you may have to increase the number of invitations you mail by 20% or so. On the other hand, some advisors feel summer is an ideal time because most of the competition is doing nothing. These seminar marketers have the field to themselves. Only you can make that determination by testing the market at least once during June, July, and August.

While there may be some regional variations concerning the best times to hold seminars, there are definitely times of the of the year seminar givers should always be aware of:

1.  Major holidays. Never plan to hold a seminar directly before or after a big holiday. This gets particularly tricky beginning with Thanksgiving. Ideally, you want to give your seminar one week, have the first appointment the second week, and have the second appointment the third week; ending with a close. The holidays at the end of the year interrupt that flow, and that flow is critical to building momentum.

2.  The very beginning of the year. Seminar attendance is usually low the first week or two of each year. Prospects have already been out to their share of evening parties and seem inclined to stay at home and recuperate.

3.  The three weeks prior to tax season, (unless you have a tax-based practice in which you give out discount coupons for tax preparation at your seminars or appointments). Then, late March and early April become a goldmine.

4.  Spring break. Even though you may be marketing to retirees, for some inexplicable reason attendance is low during this period – especially if you live in the north.

You should also be keenly aware of local events, like fairs, concerts and sporting events. If they take place during the week, you should consider how it could affect your seminar attendance. Finally, it probably goes without saying, but never ever hold a seminar on a weekend.

Advisors should focus on the good times of the year for seminars. Early fall and early spring tend to be planning times for most people. These are the times when people want to get out socializing and networking. Research has shown that the autumn months of September and October and the spring months of April and May are the best for seminars. Winter months are still fine; just be sure you make arrangements with the venue for alternate dates in case of inclement weather.

Generally, the best days of the week to hold seminars are thought to be Tuesday, Wednesday, and Thursday. But this is not a hard and fast rule. Your location will play a part in your decision. In some parts of the country many people attend events at their church on Wednesday nights. Thursday seminars can present a problem with booking your appointments. If you do most of your appointment setting by telephone the day after the seminar, Thursday events give you only one day to reach attendees before the weekend. Remember, the closer to the seminar you are when trying to get people into your office, the better. Your prospects will cool off considerably if you have to wait until Monday to try to reach them again. In spite of conventional advice, there is nothing wrong with giving a seminar on a Monday.

Choosing the best time of day is the trickiest of all. First of all, you should be aware that in most parts of the country dinner seminars outdraw lunches by at least a two to one ratio. Frankly, the thinking among prospects is: "Why should I go for a small lunch when I can have a three course dinner instead?"

Here is how to choose the best time for your seminars if your target is seniors. First take into account what time full darkness falls. Then plan on serving dinner 45 minutes prior to that time. The cardinal rule of all seminars is, never feed people until after you have delivered the presentation. So, assume you will be giving a one-hour presentation prior to dinner. Theoretically, now you have the best starting time for your event. Notice the word "theoretically". If you are marketing to younger seniors or baby boomers that may not yet be retired, make sure your event doesn't conflict with their work schedule.

Scheduling the timing of your seminars is the best place to start testing the variables in your invitation, and you should start testing with your very first invitation mailing. Even though many seminar companies suggest setting four dates, start with three. Put two of the seminars at the same time of day and make one a little earlier or later. See if there are any differences in the number or quality of attendees. It may take a few tries to get optimum results. Of course, this test assumes you are using the same venue for all your events. If you are trying to test both location and time, you won't be able to determine which variable caused the results to change.

In addition to deciding what time to serve dinner, there is another timing element to consider. This has to do with choosing when to give your seminars each month. It is a good practice to schedule your seminar dates in week blocks, separated by a week in-between. For instance, schedule Tuesday and Thursday events in week #1 and week #3, leaving week #2 and week #4 for initial appointments and follow-up. If you are booking appointments by phone, your seminar coordinator needs time to do this without having to worry about making seminar confirmation calls at the same time.

To determine the scheduling for mailing your invitations, figure that prospects should receive the invitation 10 days prior to the first seminar date listed on your invitation. Your seminar marketing company should accurately advise you regarding lead time.

Spreading out your seminar dates has other benefits as well. If bad weather has set in, it will have time to pass. If the prospect has guests or is on vacation, you have a better chance that they will still be able to attend on one of your dates that month. If they are sick, they will have time to get well.

Make sure you have also privately set aside a date and time for any overflow, or in case nasty weather affects one of your other dates. Unfortunately, when you have to change the date of an event, you generally lose about 25% of the attendees. If this happens, be sure to book these people right away for the following month or for your overflow date if you have a large enough crowd.

Over time, you will develop a system that is right for you and your market.

# Staffing Your Event

If you decide to hire a seminar coordinator, you are looking for a Jack or Jill of all trades. The question is whether to hire a full-time seminar coordinator or select a member of your staff to take on the additional workload. Financial considerations are one way to decide. Although the salary varies throughout the country, the position usually pays in the neighborhood of $30k a year plus bonuses for each appointment set and kept.

The person who is responsible for assisting you in your seminar endeavors must know how to manage a database. He or she will be responsible for using that database to follow up seminar bookings and appointments, as well as deleting attendees who have not made an appointment within a period of time following the seminar.

The coordinator must also have the ability to oversee the creation and assembly of all the components in your handout package. This requires superb attention to detail and follow-through.

The ability to work a flexible schedule is critical. Approximately 80% of all seminars are given after work hours. Your seminar coordinator needs to be present before the beginning of each seminar, and stay until the last attendee has left. This can sometimes be as late as eight or nine o' clock in the evening.

Your coordinator will need to act as the liaison with the seminar venue. It takes a strong, professional personality to deal with the restaurant staff and management, especially when resolving set-up problems and last minute changes.

He or she will likely have a close working relationship with your seminar marketing company as well. Again, this requires skill in utilizing databases and staying on top of all details regarding attendance, because each extra meal is costing you money. After you have given three or four seminars, you would be wise to call the seminar marketing company privately and ask for an honest assessment of how well your employee is doing.

The person you choose must not only be highly personable with attendees at the seminar, but have excellent phone skills as well. In all probability they will be making the seminar confirmation calls before the event. Those advisors who elect to book appointments the day after the seminar may decide to use the seminar coordinator for this task too. Sometimes people sound completely different on the telephone than they do in person. Give your prospective employee a telephone test by asking them to book a first appointment with you as a potential client who attended a seminar. Appointment setting is a difficult job at best. It is not for the shy or timid. It is also not for someone who tends to procrastinate. Every day lost by failure to book appointments is critical to your bottom line.

The ability to set up, organize, and oversee the entire seminar is a vital part of this job; which makes for some unusual requirements. If you are hiring somebody new for your seminars, find out if they have a fairly large car. While this question may sound strange and overly intrusive, there is a good reason behind it. They need to be able to transport all the equipment to the site ahead of your arrival. This involves being able to transport a large screen for your PowerPoint® presentation, unless there is one available on site at no extra charge.

This new employee cannot be a technophobe as they will need to be able to connect all the presentation elements such as your computer, sound, projector, and lighting well in advance, without outside help. This person should also be your technical trouble-shooter if something goes wrong during your presentation. This allows you to continue with your presentation seamlessly while the problem is corrected.

Because you want your presentation to be a special event, your staff needs to dress accordingly. Visual cues say a great deal about your practice. Just as you will be wearing your favorite suit to make a good impression, so should your employees. Based on your coordinator's salary, you may want to provide a reasonable clothing allowance for a couple of outfits to be worn only at seminars.

Because your seminar coordinator will be the person greeting guests at the sign in table -- and the first member of your team your prospects see -- appearance is important. Hopefully the bonding process with your attendees will have already started over the telephone during the seminar confirmation calls. In other words, you want to hire an extrovert.

The most difficult part of selecting a seminar coordinator is finding a person who can deliver a knockout introduction. This is a speaker who has enough charisma to quiet the audience and focus all their attention on you. Because the best introductions involve a heartfelt endorsement of you and your practice, sincerity means everything.

If you are hiring someone new, ask the prospective employee to present an impromptu introduction of him or herself. This is certainly putting someone on the spot. But that is precisely the point. You want someone who performs well under pressure.

It is helpful to have an additional woman at the event to act as a hostess. Her job will be to seat the attendees after they are registered and make them feel welcome. She should offer to get attendees a beverage while they are waiting and periodically make the rounds of the tables to see if everyone is comfortable. Your seminar coordinator will be too busy at the sign in table to perform these duties.

However, when it is time for the presentation to begin, your hostess will take over the job of registering attendees while your seminar coordinator gives your introduction. Your hostess can also help out with duties during the break and with the collection of appointment cards at the end of your speech. Having the additional help of a hostess at your event will allow you time to get everything perfect for your presentation. Remember, you don't get a second chance to make a first impression.

# Promoting Your Event

We have all heard the old adage, "If a tree falls in the forest and no one is around to hear it, does it make a sound?" This concept is a perfect way to view seminar marketing. You can have the best presentation, at the best venue, with the best meal, on the nicest day of the year. But if your best prospects don't know about it, you will have the worst event ever.

Promoting your seminar is the most important aspect of a successful event. Simply running an ad in a local newspaper is not going to maximize your potential for getting in front of your best prospect. While many financial advisors choose to handle this activity in-house as way to save, they would be well advised to hire a seminar marketing company to handle this activity.

A qualified seminar marketing company will give you the edge you need to have a successful seminar event. When selecting a company, make certain that they have experience with general public financial seminars. Make sure that they have worked with financial "top producers" and get at least three non-competing references. Call the references. Ask what their experience has been with the company and most important, what response rate they have experienced as a result of their marketing.

Once you have settled on a seminar marketing company, don't be afraid to let them guide you through the process. A competent firm will have worked with hundreds of advisors and can suggest the best way to promote your event to your desired target market.

Most successful seminar marketers utilize a seminar invitation that is delivered to their prospect by mail. This will allow you to specifically target your audience by any number of demographic criteria. Newspaper and radio advertising expose your event to a wide audience for a very finite period of time but do not give you the ability to target the audience nearly as well. The seminar invitation gives your prospect the sense that he has been selected and invited to the event based on his personal financial circumstances. Other forms of advertising do not convey this sense of exclusivity. If fact, they destroy it.

A carefully crafted, compliance approved, invitation is your best tool to attract financially pre-qualified prospects.

The size and geographical diversity of your target market will determine the number of invitations you will need to mail to reach your desired result. Most seminar marketers in metropolitan markets will mail 5,000 to 7,000 invitations to fill up to three events. The size of your venue also factors into the equation. Again, a competent seminar marketing company can help you determine the size of your target audience and the quantity to mail.

The cost of seminar invites can vary greatly. On the surface, you might be inclined to use a simple, less expensive piece to minimize cost. When evaluating which invitation to use, focus your cost analysis based on "cost per prospect" instead of "cost per invitation". For example, you may be initially attracted to an invitation that costs 50¢ per piece verses one that costs 75¢ per piece. After all, a savings of 25¢ on a total mailing of 5,000 pieces is $1,250. Ask your seminar marketing company what their response rates are for both invitation styles when directed to your target market.

If the cheaper invite generates a .75% response and the more costly invite yields a 1.5% response, the more expensive piece will result in a lower cost per prospect. The more costly invite delivers a cost per prospect of $50 while the cost per prospect from the cheaper invite is $67.

This is not to say that the lower cost invite will always produce the lower cost. It just depends on your event and your target audience.

While seminar marketing can be a bit of a numbers game, pure numbers are not what you are looking for. The quality of your prospects will also factor into your success. Remember, your goal is to attract financially qualified prospect that have the desire to work with you. The way your invitation is structured can have a profound impact on the type of prospective clients you attract. Your seminar marketing company can help you work through your compliance department to create an invitation that appeals to your best prospects.

# Handling Reservations

When a prospect picks up the telephone to reserve seats at your upcoming seminar, you should regard this as your first point of sale. In an attempt to save money, many advisors use their office number on the invitation and rely on an answering machine after hours and on weekends. Most people hate talking to a machine. In fact, some hate it so much they will simply hang up. Since the cost of an RSVP service is relatively insignificant when measured against the total cost of a seminar, trying to handle reservations yourself is truly a false economy.

There are several reasons to hire an outside firm rather than using your own staff. If you leave the reservations up to an employee whose primary job function is something else, there is no doubt some attendees will fall through the cracks. Your seminar coordinator may not be able to pick up each and every call. Someone else who takes the call may have no idea if a particular date is already full, or might fail to pass on the reservation to your seminar coordinator. This is a recipe for disaster. All phone calls must come in through one central booking person or service.

The quality of RSVP services varies greatly. To find a good one, start by asking your seminar marketing company. Be aware that some of these firms also own the reservation service so you need to ask for additional referrals as well. Once you have selected your service and have received your own toll-free number, make sure to test the number – and the service - before any invitations are actually printed. Do this by calling your number at three different times of day on three different days of the week. This will not only let you know how professional the service sounds on the phone, but whether or not your number has a dedicated operator during and after business hours.

Never choose a reservation company that gives your prospects a code to use instead of an 800 number. Having to locate a special code on your invitation will not only irritate your prospect; you will find that less than half will be able to locate the code and convey it correctly. Either way, you lose a prospect.

It is also a mistake for the operator to pretend they are part of your own office staff, even though that may be tempting. Frequently, callers ask questions about your firm that will reveal that the operator is not in your office. You do not want to get caught in a misrepresentation. Instead, have the operator tell each attendee that the seminar coordinator will be calling them back to reconfirm and answer any special questions.

The reason for the callback is threefold. First, it gives you a great opportunity to bond with the prospect. Second, you can ensure all questions are answered correctly. And third, it allows you to keep the initial call to the RSVP service short. You will need a number of questions answered by the attendees regarding their phone number and address, as well as those of their guests. Your office should be in charge of gathering all that information for your seminar tracking sheets. Also if you are able to offer a choice of entrée, you can do this at the same time. Just remember that the call back should be immediate whenever possible. It should also be followed up by the seminar confirmation letter you will find in the appendix.

If you are unable to make the confirmation calls from your own office, including the ones right before the event, most RSVP services will do that for a small charge. In general, you will be charged anywhere from $150 to $300 for setting up your RSVP service. After that, some companies charge by the month and some by the number of calls. In return, you should expect to be given a link to a private web page that displays your guests for each event during the period covered by the invitation. Some companies will also send you daily lists of attendees on an Excel® spreadsheet.

It is absolutely vital to provide the RSVP service with a written list of instructions for every mailing. The reason for this is that you may be using different venues with different seating capacities. They should know if your cutoff number is absolute or if you can squeeze in a few extras. It is also important to give the company exact instructions on how to handle any overflow. Do you want those guests to go to any other seminar or one date in particular? You never want to simply turn a prospect away without giving them an option to attend other events. If you require a minimum number of attendees in order to hold an event, you will also need to tell the RSVP service how to handle a date with very few bookings. Also give the company instructions on how late they can accept a booking on a certain date. That will usually depend upon the policy of the restaurant and how well they can deal with extra meals at the last minute. (Most seminar marketers assume a 10% no-show rate to avoid paying for extra meals.)

If you have any unresolved problems with the service you are getting from your seminar reservation company, the first thing you should do is tell the seminar marketing company that recommended them. They will have a great deal of leverage over the RSVP service because they provide numerous referrals to them annually. They do not want to hear you are unhappy with their recommendation. Getting reservations right and sounding professional are vital first steps in your seminar process. Don't settle for anything less than the best.

# Before Your Presentation

It is important that the person responsible for setting up your event arrives at the venue well in advance. He or she should be carrying with them a copy of their contract with the venue, which should include a diagram of the room layout, as well as one of two lists of seminar attendees.

Chances are good that the room will not be set up to your exact specifications when you arrive, and you cannot begin your work until the venue's staff corrects it. It is imperative to always have a copy of the layout with you to resolve any conflicts quickly.

When you arrive, take a look around the parking lot to see if there will be adequate parking and it is free of debris. Walk into the building as if you were a seminar attendee. Are the entrance and corridors clean and inviting? If not, have the venue's staff correct any problems. Do you need extra signage so people can locate your event easily?

Once you get into the room, make sure all the lighting and the electrical outlets are working so you can plug in all your components.

Make sure you have a free-standing podium in place and that it is well lit without interfering with the screen. A podium is extremely helpful. It is the place where you begin and end your seminar and the place you go to when you wish to change topics or make an important point. A printout of your PowerPoint® slides and your commentary should be at the podium along with a clock, a pitcher of water and a glass. The reason for the last two will become apparent in the chapter on giving your presentation.

Next, set up your screen for your PowerPoint® presentation. Test all the seats in the house to make sure the screen can be seen from each one. This is also the time to make sure the table for the projector is perfectly situated.

After that, you should be ready to work with the rest of your tables. If you are using rounds, they should be set with empty places so nobody has their back to the speaker. If you have to use oblong tables in an open "U", leave space at the junctures to allow better access and ease feelings of claustrophobia. Again, nobody should have their back to you.

If there is space in the room, your contract should call for a six or eight foot "break table". This is where you place all the beverages that are to be offered prior to the event and during any break. It should be skirted and decorated with an appropriate centerpiece to lend a festive mood. Don't forget to ask for a garbage can that will fit underneath the table so the assistant can clear away the clutter during the course of the evening.

You should also request that four to six chairs be placed next to the entry door. These are reserved for late arrivals who can then take a place at the tables during the break.

Don't forget to set up one table at the back of the room with a special reserved sign. This is where you will seat attendees with special needs or ones you worry may become troublesome. For example, if a person is hard of hearing or not fluent in English, they may have brought an interpreter. It will be much less disruptive to the presentation if they are placed at the back of the room rather than in the middle of everybody. This is also the table where you seat guests who are not on your RSVP list and where the seminar coordinator is seated during the presentation. That way, she can deal discretely with any difficult or unusual situations. This also gives her the best access to cue the venue staff before the break and before the end of the seminar.

If your seminars are not full and you find yourself talking over empty chairs to people huddled at the back of the room, that problem is easily solved by using reserved signs on all the tables. Have your hostess take the attendees to the tables at the front of the room, remove the reserved signs, and say, "We have saved a special place for you where you can see and hear everything better." This way you can fill the front of the room first. By the way, since all attendees should be wearing nametags, it is also the job of the hostess to introduce people as she seats them at the tables. This takes away the feeling of intrusion attendees feel when they sit down at a table filled with strangers.

Now it is time to make sure your sound system is in order. However, wait to do the voice level checks until the person who is giving the introductions and the advisor arrive. It is extremely helpful to set a relaxed mood by playing music prior to the presentation, during the break, and during dinner. Stopping the music also lets people know when they should be in their seats and quiet for times when someone is addressing the audience.

You should, at this point, tape down all the cords for safety and hide all excess cords for appearances sake. And speaking of appearances, hopefully the venue has provided all your tables with small centerpieces or candles which should be lit during dinner.

Now that the inside of your room is taking shape, your skirted sign in table and a chair should be in place right outside. Place your easel and framed sign next to the entryway. You will want to have your seminar handout folders placed in front of you in alphabetical order according to the attached nametags. Don't forget an additional supply of blank name tags along with pens. Of course, the most important thing you will need is your seminar sign in sheet. Make sure it is in alphabetical order and check with the reservation company two hours before the event to ensure your names and numbers are correct.

If you have not already done so, talk with the venue's manager to find out how much lead time they need before the break to restock the break table, and how much lead time they need to begin preparing the meals. That way, the seminar coordinator can time the cues properly. By this time, the staff should have all the tables set with a small bowl of snacks on each table.

About 45 minutes prior to the event you are in the final countdown. This means the advisor should have arrived and all speakers, (the person making the introductions and the presenter), can do their sound checks. The speaker should also make sure his computer and projector are working properly for the PowerPoint® presentation.

Ask the staff to do a final vacuum of the room and the entrances. Meanwhile, check the restrooms to make sure they are spotless. As you walk around outside, you will no doubt notice that a few attendees have arrived extra early. This is particularly true if you are working with retirees. Make sure they have a comfortable place to sit and wait until you open the doors about 30 minutes before the start of the event.

Seniors often chill easily so this is the time to begin to adjust the temperature in the room to about 75 degrees. However, enlist your assistant to keep checking prior to the seminar to see if the temperature is agreeable to your attendees.

Now is the time to set the mood by turning on some soft music while the restaurant staff begins filling the water glasses. Remember that you want your own staff to bond with the attendees at every opportunity. This is the reason to have your hostess bring them a beverage from the break table prior to the presentation and pass out cookies or other treats during the break.

At 30 minutes before the start of the event, everyone and everything should be in place. You are now ready to open the doors and to begin signing attendees in. Since people often arrive in clusters, you need to avoid delays. This is not the time to fill in missing information because you can do that during the break. If you need to take care of parking validation, have that set up at a separate side table and enlist the help of someone from the venue, if possible.

If you have the resources and the know-how, creating a brief slide loop that plays while people are waiting is an extra, thoughtful touch. It can be a combination of scenic photos, your credentials and designations, and, (if compliance will allow it), testimonials from enthusiastic clients.

Some advisors prefer to make their first appearance right after the introduction. Others prefer to welcome their guests prior to the presentation. The latter method is the better choice. It enables you to both warm up and size up the audience. If you can develop a certain rapport with one or two of the attendees in such a short period, you now have people to go to for positive eye contact during your presentation. You can also take care of all the niceties such as thanking people for coming ahead of time.

As the time to start the seminar approaches, dim the lights and turn off the music. You are now ready to begin the best seminar of your life.

# Giving Your Presentation

There are two important things to remember when giving a seminar. The first is that you wish to evoke a complex combination of responses from the audience. By the end of your presentation you want them to respect you, trust you, feel you have the expertise to solve their particular problems, and you want them to like you enough that they can envision having a relationship with you for many years to come.

The second thing to remember is that you are there for one purpose only: to get each buying unit to book an appointment as soon as possible. You may feel your purpose is to educate and perhaps to entertain, but these outcomes are merely ancillary. Quite simply, when you give a seminar, you mean business.

Fortunately, focusing on business does not mean you have to come across as a person who utilizes a hard sell approach. Every advisor has a distinct personality. Some are reserved and unassuming, but they can use this to their advantage to project a quiet self-confidence. Others come across as technocrats. As long as they don't confuse the audience with a barrage of numbers, they can dazzle the attendees with their grasp of financial strategies. And some advisors are just naturally aggressive, but this does not mean that the audience will be put off by their forcefulness. Aggressive advisors can deliver their presentation in a way that implies, "I am strong. You can depend on me to take care of you."

Don't try to be someone you are not when you are in the spotlight. Instead, take the best parts of your personal style and emphasize them. Otherwise, the audience will sense insincerity, and insincerity erodes trust. There is one more essential word of advice about your presence on stage. Enjoy yourself! Show that you are passionate about your field and take your audience along for the ride. If you do that, you will give them an evening they are bound to remember.

The whole evening should be orchestrated until it builds to a crescendo with the close of your presentation. This means you should get the trivial issues out of the way first by using a two-tiered introduction.

Because you have stated on your invitation that the doors will close promptly at a certain time, most attendees will expect you to adhere to your timeline. Unfortunately, you will almost always have people who will arrive a bit late. (How late you are still willing to allow people to enter is a decision you should have made in advance and discussed with the hostess who will man the sign in table once the introductions have started. You need to take into account that sometimes there are special circumstances due to severe weather conditions, traffic jams, etc.) Fortunately there is a solution.

This is where the double introduction comes in. This will allow you to begin with someone speaking promptly as promised, but it will also buy you time while latecomers are still arriving. To start the evening, the person you have chosen to do your introductions should go to the podium, pick up the microphone and thank everyone for coming. This is the time for the "housekeeping speech". Never tell people what time the seminar will end, but do let them know there will be a break with light refreshments served. Advise them of the location of the restrooms and ask them to turn off their cell phones. Also ask them to raise their hands if they are either too hot or too cold. Let them know you have several freshly cleaned sweaters which you will be glad to lend to anyone who is uncomfortable. Nothing makes attendees more disgruntled than feeling like they are freezing. In addition, tell the group that you will be seated at the table at the back of the room throughout the presentation. If there is anything anyone needs, all they have to do is raise their hand and you will be more than happy to attend to them.

After the person giving the introductions has delivered the house-keeping speech, there may still be a number of empty seats. The speaker should tell the audience that a few attendees have been courteous enough to call to say they are running a bit late and you have promised to delay the presentation briefly so they can be seated. Then the speaker should sit down while you wait an additional three to five minutes. This is a good time to encourage the audience to read the seminar handouts, refresh their beverages, or let them know this is the last chance to use the facilities.

Here is another suggestion. If you have constructed a slide loop, it is wise to run it at this time. During the introduction is a good time to show a picture with the location of your office. Few things are more boring than hearing an advisor start a presentation by talking about his office and its location. If your office is not photogenic, put up a map instead.

Now that you have the practical details of the seminar out of the way, you can concentrate on the other reason for the two-tiered introduction. The purpose of this is to build excitement in the audience about the coming presentation. For those advisors who are wary of being introduced, remember one thing. Another person can brag about your accomplishments in a way that you can't without appearing pompous. This way you will be able to begin your speech with your credibility already established.

Don't wait more than six minutes after the stated starting time to give the actual introduction. This should be carefully scripted and memorized. However, it should be delivered in a conversational manner. Here is an example of the structure of an introduction that builds as it is spoken.

"It is my very great pleasure to introduce our speaker for the evening, because he comes to you with great expertise in the field of retirement planning. John Doe graduated with a degree in business from X University. After college, he used that knowledge as the vice president for the X Financial Management Firm where he was in charge of special strategies for retirement accounts. Over a decade ago, John decided he preferred to work directly with retirees, so he started his own firm, XXX. While doing this he managed to obtain his CFP. For those who are not familiar with the term, a CFP or Certified Financial Planner is a designation held by only 11% of this country's financial advisors. This is obviously a description of an overachiever. I can speak from personal experience, as I talk with our clients daily. John receives many accolades from those happy with his service, particularly with his ability to find strategies to lower their taxes. I can guarantee that he is a person well worth listening to tonight. Ladies and gentlemen, please join me in welcoming your speaker, John Doe."

The person giving the introduction should start the applause and shake hands with you, the advisor, before turning over the stage. Now you need to take complete charge of the room. Do this by taking a four second pause at the podium before speaking. This is designed to build anticipation.

Finally, it is your turn to take center stage. At this point you will have 97% of the audience's attention for the first two minutes. Their attention span will ebb and flow throughout your presentation; sometimes as low as 50% until you give your four minute close. At that point you will have regained about 95% of their attention. This is why it is so important to seize the moment when you take the stage.

If you are wearing a wireless lavaliere lapel microphone, (listed in our chapter on equipment in the appendix), it won't matter whether you are soft spoken or the loudest guy in the room. The important thing is to take ownership of the seminar. Remember that confident body language is critical. Experts say it accounts for over 90% of the audience's perception of you.

Always "welcome" the audience instead of thanking them for attending. Your seminar coordinator or assistant has already done that. By issuing a welcome, you have immediately taken the leadership role and made it a positive one. Everyone knows this is your event.

You want to begin with a powerhouse declaration, such as, "As I look out over this audience tonight, I realize that three out of every four of you are going to outlive your nest egg." Or if you are truly confident, you can start by saying, "I want each and every one of you to make an appointment with me tonight because I can guarantee I will save you money."

This is the time to be bold. It is not the time to discuss the weather, the traffic, the location of your office, or any other mundane subjects. Don't begin with a joke because the audience may not find it funny, and you will be met with deafening silence. You should never tell jokes anyway. Use anecdotes instead because they are safe, and they should be relevant enough to emphasize the point you are making. It is also unwise to ask a rhetorical question at the beginning of your presentation in case no one responds. For instance, "Does everyone here want to save money on their taxes?" These are all frequently used attempts aimed at bonding with the audience. But that is something that cannot be rushed. You need to earn their respect first because that is the only way they will continue listening to you. And you can't sell them if they aren't paying attention.

At the end of your own two or three minute introduction about the presentation, it is time to introduce your appointment sheets. They should be printed in a different color from the rest of your handouts so they are easy for attendees to locate. Hold one up and ask the audience to pull theirs out of their welcome packet. Let the audience know that you will be covering a great number of valuable strategies during the evening. Encourage them to put a check mark beside each topic which interests them. This will give the audience an extra degree of involvement. It will also be a great reference you can utilize in booking appointments and preparing for the first appointment. Refer to your appointment sheet several times during your presentation. There should also be a space on your sheet where attendees can list additional topics that interest them. Obviously, if a particular subject occurs repeatedly, you may wish to include it in future presentations. But remember, all you want to do is deliver just enough information to entice your audience to book an appointment.

The beginning of your presentation is also the time to let people know how you intend to handle questions. Although answering questions can demonstrate your financial expertise, you can make better use of them by saying you will answer everybody's questions during their free consultation.

No doubt you have been told you need to make eye contact with as many people in the room as possible. If you are uncomfortable or nervous at the outset, try this technique. Scan the audience and you will always find several people who are on your side. Perhaps these are some of the attendees you spoke with personally prior to your presentation. These are your "partisans". Your partisans will often smile openly at you and will not break eye contact when you look in their direction. Often these friendly audience members will nod in agreement as you make key points. Find your partisans and speak to them often. They will tend to bond further with you, and you will gain support from them. After you speak to a partisan, make a point of addressing someone nearby, changing that person every time you complete a cycle. This will keep you from scanning the audience or doing what is called "lighthousing". Lighthousing occurs when the speaker keeps sweeping his eyes quickly back and forth across the room in a feeble attempt to make eye contact with every participant. It will weaken your presentation.

Learn to use your voice like a fine instrument. You can do this in several ways: speed up or slow down the pacing, speak loudly for emphasis or softly so the audience will be forced to listen intently, pause for a few seconds, or reiterate an important point and vary the pitch. All these suggestions take some practice to do well, but they will keep you from giving your delivery in monotone. On another note, keep to the schedule you have set for yourself. Nobody has ever complained that a seminar was too short.

The most successful presenters make a point of coming out from behind the podium and standing with their feet slightly spread, (ten inches apart for men and six inches apart for women). This is known as a "power stance" by experts on body language. The best speakers also frequently walk into the audience as they speak. When audience members answer genuine questions correctly, the speaker recognizes them and congratulates them publicly.

Nobody goes to a financial seminar expecting a floorshow. Don't feel obligated to entertain your guests. They will receive sufficient reward from your good financial advice and a free meal. You definitely want to appear confident and relaxed; because if you are relaxed, your audience will relax right along with you and be more receptive to your message.

There are a few tricks you can do to relax yourself. One is to lean your elbow on the podium for a couple of minutes while you are speaking. However, never employ this technique while you are making an important point. Some advisors place a stool on one side of the stage and sit on it while they are talking from time to time. Near the end of your seminar, you can even loosen your tie a little. However, never remove your suit jacket.

Every advisor fears losing his place or forgetting what comes next. This is the only time you can get away with turning around and reading your PowerPoint®. But make it look like a deliberate act done for emphasis. You can also cover your lapse by rubbing your eyes, shuffling papers on the podium or simply staring at the floor for a few seconds.

If you look again at the equipment list, you will notice it calls for a pitcher of water and a glass. There are two reasons these items are on this list. You can cover a momentary lapse of memory by pouring yourself a glass of water and taking a drink from it. All these devices that help you recover from forgetfulness serve a dual purpose. They should be used occasionally even if your memory is perfect. Here is the explanation of the theatrics: Your audience can only concentrate on the most difficult parts of the presentation for very limited periods of time. You can use these devices for breaks in your speech to allow their brains time to catch up. Also remember that there is nothing wrong in asking the audience directly, "Is everybody with me?"

Neuroscientists have figured out that the average brain can concentrate deeply for a maximum of 23 minutes. Because of this, you should take a five-minute break right before you tackle your most complex subject. You may consider that break a waste of time, and wish to power on through to the end. However, this period gives you another chance to bond with your audience.

Your presentation should drive people to action. You want to show the audience the reward for action and the penalty for inaction. Illustrate these concepts by using personal anecdotes from your practice. During the first half it is best to employ stories that talk about your clients and what you have done to rescue them. However, at the halfway point you should begin to change your illustrations.

Now you need to set yourself up for your close. As you move closer to the end of your presentation, your stories should instead illustrate what you have been able to accomplish for those people who have come in for their free appointment. That way, when you actually make the offer of the free appointment, your audience will be more predisposed to take advantage of it. Remember that bonding with your audience is an emotional act. They will respond better to true stories than to all the facts and figures you can throw at them. Always be sure that the stories you use are your own. There is a well known anecdote about a woman named Pat who was able to vacation in Hawaii on the taxes the advisor saved on her social security. Advisors who used this tale would even hold up a postcard with a picture of a tropical paradise and claim it was a thank you from Pat. There must have been, at one time, at least four hundred advisors across the country using the same presentation and the postcard from Pat. One can easily assume that many seminar attendees heard the very same "personal story".

As you move towards your close, never tell the audience that you are nearing completion. If you do, they will start looking at their watches and wondering how soon dinner will be served. In fact, never tell your audience in advance the length of the seminar. Do not look at your watch, but instead at the clock hidden on the podium. You should not mention time at all. Instead surprise them by moving seamlessly into the discussion of your offer of a free appointment.

A slide of your appointment sheet should come up on your PowerPoint® at the end of your seminar. This is where you reiterate the promise you have made to cover relevant topics. The mistake most advisors make is to go on and on during the close. You should keep it brief, powerful, and to the point. Most importantly, end with a compelling declarative sentence, and STOP TALKING! This is the time to get them writing on their appointment cards.

Every advisor should try at least once to book appointments during the close at the seminar while the attendees are the most motivated. At the very least you should pick up one or two prospects that you might not have otherwise gotten. The next chapter tells you how to do exactly that.

# Turning Prospects
# Into Clients

# Setting Appointments

You will never have more trust from your audience than the trust you have earned at the close of your seminar. Set appointments on site before that trust has a chance to fade away.

Your assistant should collect the appointment cards from each attendee as quickly as possible. You can move that process along by letting the audience know that the meal will be served once all cards are collected. Your seminar coordinator next should write down all specific appointment requests on your calendar and give appointment cards to the attendees who have made a commitment.

Meanwhile you should make the rounds of each table in order to encourage questions. When a question is asked, you should say that you would prefer to answer it in private during the course of the free appointment. Use the assumptive approach, and if the prospect has not booked an appointment, sound surprised and call over the seminar coordinator to set the day and time and make a record of their question. If they have a specific question to be answered, be sure to include it in your first appointment letter.

Some advisors prefer to set appointments by telephone. If so, never let a weekend pass without making several attempts to contact attendees and set an appointment. Begin calling at 9:00 AM the day after your seminar. You can call as late as 7:00 PM in the evening; just be sure to ask first if you are interrupting dinner.

Call each and every attendee and thank them for coming. Try to open a conversation before asking for an appointment. Ask them first of all how they enjoyed the meal. They will feel obliged to say they liked it, and you should have your first positive opening. Even though you will have the appointment cards in your hand, with topics of interest checked, do not begin by asking your prospects if there were any financial strategies that interested them. Ask instead if there were any stories that hit home. Get them to talk about themselves before suggesting they come to your office for a no-obligation appointment. If that doesn't elicit a meeting, bring up the topics they checked off on their cards or any questions they might want answered. This is one reason it is better for the advisor to set appointments instead of the seminar coordinator, who will not be able to elicit specific financial concerns.

Don't leave a voice message unless you feel you have no other options. Once you leave a message, you will have fewer opportunities to call the prospect again if you receive no response. Attempt to call at least three different times of day before leaving a voice message.

Appointment ratios are usually best if the advisor himself makes the call to prospects who have attended his seminar. Attendees are more likely to appreciate and feel obligated to the person who provided dinner. Above all, don't delay. Prospects may forget you and most of what you said if they are not contacted immediately.

# The First Appointment

The success of your first appointment depends as much upon your listening skills as it does on your skills as a speaker. Every person who enters your office comes in with a financial history, both literally and emotionally. Some prospects have attitudes about money that go back as far as childhood, and they still affect how financial decisions are made decades later. Some attitudes are also generated by external events. For example, clients who lived through the great depression tend to invest more conservatively than members of the baby boom generation.

The first appointment is your opportunity to learn as much as possible about each prospect. Even seemingly insignificant details may yield clues as to which strategies will make them the most comfortable, and how to best explain these strategies. When you get to this level of personal interaction in your office, you cannot afford to do anything that will raise doubts about your ability or your character.

If you acquired these prospects from a seminar, you should assume they are attending seminars given by other advisors as well. This puts you in a highly competitive situation. Keep in mind you are in the business of breaking relationships before you can build new ones. The first relationship you have to erode is the one your prospective clients have with their current advisor. They must see you as a preferable alternative to the person they are working with now. But you must also keep them from creating a new relationship with your competition. You do this by making every person who enters your office feel they are your sole priority.

The experience a prospective client has when entering your office will set the tone for the meeting. You want them to be in a relaxed and receptive mood. This means keeping the seating area as far away from the receptionist's desk as practical so they will not overhear her telephone conversations. Privacy is essential; so be sure that those seated in the waiting room can not hear any talking emanating from within your office. If necessary, you can solve these problems by playing some soft music.

Clutter often seems to pile up on receptionists' desks. Invest in a piece of cabinetry so they can keep things out of sight. This goes for your office and conference room as well. Limit your personal accessories to one or two photos of your family, diplomas, and framed certificates of professional designations. However, you do not want to show off your sales prowess. If you are a member of the Million Dollar Roundtable, your office is not the place to highlight it. Also make sure that any doors your clients will pass on their way to their appointment are kept closed.

While people are waiting in your lobby, they will need something interesting to read. What could be better than a client appreciation book full of testimonials and pictures taken at client events? The one thing you do not want displayed is any financial product literature. That should be reserved for you to hand out during your second or third appointments.

Always greet prospective clients in the lobby. On the way to your office, be sure to introduce your assistant. This will be helpful once your prospect becomes a client, because your assistant can handle many questions without the client calling you directly.

If you are using a table instead of a desk, always allow the clients to select where they would like to sit. Also ask if they prefer to have the door open or closed. Closed doors make some people feel trapped; others like privacy.

It is essential that you take the leadership role. However, you need to do so in a manner that is not threatening. You need to let each person know that you are truly glad they have come to see you. Before each meeting, go over the prospect's seminar appointment card to familiarize yourself with which topics they have checked. That way if they are the silent type, things needn't be awkward. The card gives you a basis for starting a discussion. Even though you are armed with their card, first ask your prospects if there is anything in particular that brought them in to see you. Find out what they expect from the meeting. Be sure to reiterate that there will be no charge and give them an idea of how long the meeting will last.

Before you begin the meeting in earnest, ask if your assistant may make a copy of the documents they have brought. This way you will have time to acquire their paperwork during the general conversation period before you get down to financial details. Unfortunately you may find that the couple has failed to bring in all the tax returns, annuities, lists of stocks and bonds, insurance policies and other items you have requested. There are many advisors who end the meeting at this point because they feel there is nothing they can do without having the necessary paperwork. But the primary purpose of the first meeting is to get a second meeting. You can still gather a great deal of information by asking pertinent questions and requesting that your prospects bring all their papers the next time. While this requires you to conduct at least three appointments, it may be justified based on your cost to acquire new prospects.

While some advisors prefer the "Let's get right down to business" approach and pull out the client asset questionnaire immediately, doing this may cause you to miss out on some valuable information that could be helpful as the appointment progresses. Your prospects may also feel they are being rushed, so take some time to get to know them. If you are not comfortable with small talk, here are some hints: Don't ask if they had trouble finding your office or talk about the weather outside. Instead get them involved in telling stories about themselves. If you are interviewing a couple, ask them to tell you how they met and how long they have been married. This question may reveal whether they are in a first or second marriage. Find out about their children and grandchildren. You may learn that there are estate-planning issues. How does the world feel different today from when they were growing up? Do they sound unduly fearful of risk? Do they have any wishes that are still unfulfilled? Perhaps you can provide more income to help make their dreams come true.

After the opening conversation, it is finally time to concentrate on business. When you do start to concentrate on the client asset questionnaire, try not to do so abruptly. This should be a conversation, not an interrogation. Even though you are filling out paperwork, keep maintaining eye contact with both parties. If for some reason you need to use a white board during the first meeting, never turn your back to them. If you want them to complete a risk tolerance form, do not leave them alone to do it. You may be needed to explain some portions of the document.

Your process should be one of interspersing fact-finding questions with emotional hooks. Find out what worries them most about the future, particularly as far as their loved ones are concerned. It might be the necessity of residing in a nursing home or having to endure a lowered standard of living. It is worth repeating what was written in a previous chapter. Women have a very real fear of abandonment. They know the statistics on longevity point towards widowhood. They want an advisor they can trust in lieu of their husbands to take good care of their money. Men also fear abandonment but in a different manner. They require help with the day-to-day care they need like cooking and housekeeping. One way to phrase abandonment issues is to ask the question of each partner, "How would you be prepared to carry on should you find yourself alone?"

Also ask whom they are investing for. It might be for themselves, or it might be for their children or grandchildren. In rare cases it might even be for charity. You can't do any kind of financial planning unless you know the answer to this basic question.

Many advisors are uncomfortable with asking direct questions about health. But not doing so is a disservice to your clients who may well need to budget for long term care. There may also be current health issues, such as prescription drugs, that are making enormous demands on their income.

You also want to ask if they are anticipating any sizable inheritances which will benefit their financial future. Likewise, you need to know if they face caring for an aged parent with no resources of their own.

By the end of the meeting, you should not only have filled out their asset and liabilities form, you should also know what they consider the necessities and what they consider the luxuries of life. You want to tap into their hopes and dreams as well as solving the problem of meeting their day-to-day living expenses. Is there anything they yearn for? Ask if they would enjoy taking a cruise, or if they want to see their grandchildren more often. Give them images that will evoke positive emotions. As your prospects discuss these things, share their enthusiasm.

You can show your excitement by mirroring their body language. If they lean forward, you lean forward. If they nod, you nod back in acknowledgement. Make them feel you are their trusted advisor and you are going to do everything you can to make their dreams come true. No doubt you will encounter many couples who do not have the resources to make their dreams possible. This does not mean that it is impossible to tap into their emotions. In these cases they may be grateful just for the gift of some degree of financial security.

No matter what your prospects' financial situation is, always congratulate them on what they have done right. You might phrase it like this, "I can tell you have worked very hard for your money, and you have done a great job. Even during difficult times, you have managed to create a nest egg. I want to help you protect what you have worked so hard for."

Naturally they are going to want to know what this is going to cost, but don't allow yourself to be dragged into a discussion of fees too soon. Let them know they are going to have options, if that is possible. Tell them they will receive a written explanation as well as a verbal explanation of how you charge. Assure them, if you can, that your fees will probably be less than they are paying now. Tell them you will be happy to discuss fees during the next appointment when you know better which financial strategies might be appropriate.

During the course of the appointment ask your prospects what their favorite investments are and why. Find out if there is anything they are unwilling to part with. You certainly don't want to criticize anything in which they have an emotional attachment. You also need to learn who the true financial decision maker is. It may or may not be the person who does the budgeting and the bill paying. Every relationship has a balance of power that is sometimes hidden. There may be a clue if a couple comes in and says very little. They may sit there frowning with their arms folded across their chests and rarely look at each other. The problem may not be you or your first appointment techniques. There may be a financial power struggle going on -- even in a couple who has been married for decades. They may have very different agendas but do not wish to say so to an outsider. In this case you must be very careful to win both parties over. You may not be able to solve their differences, but at least be sure that in your discussions you do not inadvertently show any favoritism.

At fifty minutes into a one hour appointment, it is time to begin closing the first meeting. Start by asking if there are any topics which you have failed to cover. For you, this is the final point at which you decide whether you wish to have these prospects as clients or not. If the answer is no, you know what to do. Just do so graciously.

Finally, you should recap the first appointment before you close. Have each person affirm verbally what you have discussed and what their goals are. You might say, "I would like to see you with enough money to sustain your standard of living for the rest of your lives, or I would like to see you be able to pay for your grandchildren's education. First I need to do some specific research to determine the best possible strategy for you. That should take about a week." Say this even though you may already have the answer. You want them to feel indebted that you are going to extra trouble for them.

You don't want to offend or scare prospects into doing nothing, but if their accounts have not done well, ask if they know how their investments, including all fees, compare to the performance of the S&P over the last five years. If you see something that disturbs you in terms of safety, it is your obligation to point it out. Are they paying unnecessary taxes? You are looking for a problem you can solve to bring them back. At the very least you want to better their situation.

It is also important to let your prospects know you like them and respect them. They need to feel they can ask you any question without appearing financially illiterate. Already they are mentally judging whether you are someone they want to establish a long-term relationship with. A low key approach almost always works better than high pressure sales tactics.

Give them something to take home. Ask your assistant to put together a packet with articles on the topics of special interest to them. Include a list of references you know will give a glowing report. Hand them personal letters of recommendation from other clients who have given their approval. Do not give them any information on specific products, even if they request it. Reserve all discussion of products and strategies for the second meeting.

One frequently asked question is whether an advisor should charge for the second appointment if allowed to do so. Usually, advisors who ask for this fee, do so for one of two reasons. Some see payment of a fee as a means of ensuring that their prospects are serious. Other advisors charge if they are going to take the time to construct an elaborate financial plan. While this is certainly fair, be sure your prospects truly want a long elaborate document. Remember that you are probably competing directly with other advisors who most likely are not charging. This makes it harder for you to do so. In other words, don't do anything that sets up a barrier to a second appointment.

The easiest way to make that appointment happen is to simply pull out your calendar. Ask if the same day and time the following week is acceptable. Try to be as casual as possible. When the appointment is set, give them an appointment card and list any additional materials they need to bring on the back of the card. Finally, thank them for coming and let them know you are looking forward to meeting with them next week.

As soon as they have left, immediately dictate the notes from the meeting. Consider investing in a digital voice recorder. It will cost less than a few hundred dollars, and you can send your notes off to an inexpensive overnight transcription company like *speakwrite.com* without bothering your staff. First, give an overview of the appointment with problems to be solved. Next, put down the exact phrases your prospects have used to include in your first appointment follow up letter and the next meeting. Finally, record a list of actions to be taken by you or your staff.

The very next day, send out your follow up letter with an agenda for the next meeting. This will show them you are a professional who takes care of the details. The vast majority of your prospects should return for the second meeting. In fact, if you lose more than 10% of your qualified prospects between appointments, and you are not charging for the second meeting, you may want to consider consulting a sales coach to determine how you can improve your conversion rate. After investing so much to get prospects into your office, you want to do everything possible to make sure they become clients.

# The Second Appointment

Ideally, you have managed to set up your second appointment within one week of your first appointment so there is little opportunity for your prospects' enthusiasm to die down. They should also have received your letter laying out the agenda for your second appointment. While many advisors have their seminar coordinator call to confirm the second appointment, you will get fewer no shows or cancellations if you take the time to go through this process yourself. This time it is fine to leave a message if you don't reach them, so confirmations should not take any longer than five minutes a day. Just be sure to avoid getting into any financial discussions. Save those for their next office visit.

Preparing for the second appointment involves an exercise that may seem elementary, but if you master it, you will find the flow of all your appointments will go much more smoothly. The exercise starts with writing down all the financial products and strategies you intend to discuss. Next, write down the clearest possible definition or description of each product or service. Now go back through and time exactly how long it takes to deliver each one. Edit this list for simplicity and brevity. The next step involves testing your ability to explain the financial products and strategies you use on a daily basis to people who are financial novices. Practice until you have created wording in a few short sentences that everybody easily understands. As an example, you should be able to describe an index annuity, a stretch IRA, or the implication of the words "per stirpes" so that people get your meaning immediately. The reason for this exercise is, that while you are probably a good social communicator, you may not be a good "technical" communicator and not even realize it.

Your skill in explaining the technical strategies that come up in the second appointment in simple terms may well determine whether or not a client signs with you.

As difficult as it may be, try not to think in terms of closing. If you do, you may inadvertently convey a sense of undue pressure to your prospects. Instead, during the second appointment, think in terms of trying to transfer just a few assets. After all, once your prospect has signed the transfer papers, they have become your client. After that, you will have numerous opportunities to up sell until you eventually control all -- or at least the majority -- of their investments. The idea behind this approach is that your chances of gaining more clients, more quickly, will skyrocket.

When your prospects arrive, greet them warmly and thank them for returning. The next thing you should do is recap their first appointment using the exact wording they used during the meeting. Ask them if there is anything new or anything they forgot to mention during the first appointment. Also this is the time to request any additional paperwork you may have asked them to bring in.

No matter how dire their situation, try to sound upbeat. Make this meeting an enjoyable experience. You might start off by saying, "I have some great news for you. I indicated that I may be able to increase your monthly income. Fortunately I have been able to do just that. During the meeting today I will show you how."

Next, congratulate them again on how well they have handled their money. Even if things have gone badly, always let your prospects save face about their decisions concerning their investments.

Here is a good approach: "It is true that you have lost some money, but so did a lot of other people during that time. You were probably just following all the professional advice that was considered valid at the time."

Of course, it is highly probable that the bad advice came from their current broker. If they tell you something suspect he or she did, it is best to avoid overt criticism. Simply pause with a bewildered look and say "Really? That's interesting. Have you asked why?"

At the second meeting, your prospects will arrive at your office expecting to see something in writing, and you do not want to disappoint them. But you do wish to limit what you give them. Assume whatever they take away may be shown to others. You do not want your advice shopped around. At the beginning of the appointment, many advisors will simply hand over a multi-page report and leave the room for several minutes while the prospects try to make sense of it. This is a poor practice. Instead sit with them and explain each page. Give your most important and pressing strategies verbally. This is where your technical speaking skills come in.

It is essential to remain seated beside your prospects and carefully walk them through your brief written analysis point by point and page by page. You don't want them to misunderstand anything. If you have to, write out specifics on paper while you talk but throw the paper away afterwards. Never lose eye contact by turning around and writing on a white board. Keep everything simple and personal.

The best way to get your prospects' attention is to discuss their most pressing issues first. Address their short term issues before you address their long term issues. This may highlight a problem you can solve for them immediately.

During the course of the second appointment, you will find products or strategies that your prospects are married to. Do not try to force them out of things they are tied to emotionally at the second appointment. You will have plenty of time to make changes once they are your clients. Right now you just want to get your foot in the door.

After you have discussed solutions to their short-term problems, show that you have also done research on their long term issues. Don't give them complete strategies. Simply let them know you are thinking of long term solutions as well, and promise them their future will be in good hands. Otherwise, remaining where they are could be dangerous down the road.

Try to talk in fairly broad strokes rather than getting bogged down in minutiae. Speak in terms of repositioning, consolidation, and upgrading, instead of changing, so you do not frighten them with too many decisions at once. The only decision you need them to make now is to hire you. You also don't want to scare them with words which may be negative hot buttons. If you can, use more benign terminology. For example, a charitable remainder trust might be called a "children's trust", or an insurance application might be referred to as a simple "indication of interest".

Before you begin the close, make sure you have covered the concerns of each person. Allow plenty of time for questions and clarification. It is vitally important to be as reassuring as circumstances allow. Don't even attempt to close until you find yourself in positive territory. And don't attempt to close until you have the proper transfer paperwork ready at your side.

# Closing Techniques

There are thousand upon thousands of books and courses on how to close the sale. They encourage devices such as going in for the test close, or gaining agreement on every point. Their mantra is, "If you say it, they won't believe it, but if they say it, they will believe it."

When you ask, "Does this make sense to you?" do you really want to know; or are you just trying to hurry the sales process along? If you hurry, you will lose all the time and energy you have spent in building the prospects' trust. It is easy to pile on too much pressure too early by saying something like, "If I were to show you how to avoid taxes on your social security, would this be a basis for our doing business?"

What is wrong with such time tested language? It assumes that people choose a financial advisor based on logic rather than emotion. Furthermore, the last thing you want to do is evoke negative emotions by using obvious sales jargon. The other difficulty is that sales jargon does not conform to the way people normally speak. Red flags will go up if your phrasing suddenly begins to sound artificial.

The overworked phrase "just be yourself" truly applies to this situation. However, that doesn't mean you can't employ certain strategies.

One of the first challenges you need to overcome is your prospects' apprehension about breaking their relationship with their current broker. Everybody dreads doing this, even if they are unhappy with the advice they have been given. Let people know that they do not have to have an uncomfortable conversation, and let them know you can take care of this for them, by letter. They may be worried that their broker may still phone them in an attempt to save the account. Give your prospects the language to use if this occurs. Tell them not to burn any bridges. Instead they can say, "I have made my decision, and I would like to try it out for a few months. If I am unhappy with the change, I would like to leave the door open and come back to you, if you are comfortable with that." Now the onus is on the other advisor.

Remember that you want to be seen as a problem solver. You can do this during the close, but not by taking them through endless charts and complicated explanations. Instead, tell them the story of how you have helped a client in a situation similar to theirs. You want them to identify with the people you are using in your example. They should relate to this method of closing a whole lot better than a purely technical approach.

You need to speak with confidence. Take all the tentativeness and qualifiers out of your conversation. If the situation allows, get rid of all the "mays" and "mights" and substitute the word "will". In a close, don't say, "I think..." Say, "I am sure that..." Show your prospects that you can be a leader in helping them make the correct financial decisions.

On the other hand, when discussing products and strategies, you must tell both sides of the story by giving the pluses and minuses of each. Try to sound fair and balanced rather than overtly partisan. This does not mean you should avoid giving your opinion on which course of action should be taken.

The old adage of "sell with benefits, not with features" is true. You want to sell them the car, not tell them how the engine was built. In other words, do not allow the discussion to get bogged down or sidetracked at any point. You are in the process of building the momentum that leads to a "yes". The last thing you want to hear is, "I need to go home and think about it." Usually that is tantamount to a "no".

During the close you should have honed the decisions down to one or two options that need to be addressed immediately to avoid a potentially bad financial situation. Just as prospects should not be overwhelmed with choices, it is just as dangerous to offer only one strategy. If your prospective clients don't agree with it, you are left with nothing and nowhere to go.

Even though you are expressing a pressing need for immediate action, don't ask for too much change too soon. Instead, take the opposite approach. Insist that once their most pressing problem is solved, you don't want to do anything with the rest of the account for a while. You want to use the time to really get to know your clients first and then take measured steps over the course of the next several months. Tell them you will be very systematic and deliberate in your approach. Also, you want to meet with and get input from other advisors such as their attorney and CPA.

Give a description of how everything will work. "It will take about three weeks to get everything transferred over, after that we are going to sit down together and review everything with outside input if necessary. Then we will make one of the small changes we have decided should be implemented immediately. During the first few months with a new client, I like to meet frequently on a regular basis so I can be sure you are completely comfortable with any additional upgrades or repositioning."

You are now into the final portion of your close. You should be sure by this point that you have not asked prospects to buy into your belief system too soon. They have got to truly believe in you. They have to like you and trust you. They must also be aware of why they should do business only with you. In other words, you should have articulated what is often referred to as your unique value proposition.

If you can say this honestly, try these words: "This product (or strategy) is what I have used with my mother (myself, or other relative). I know it will work equally well for you." Of course, this is not a suggestion to use these words if they are untrue.

You will win people over by expressing optimism and your desire to work with them. In fact, you are eager to get started making their lives better. If you sense any negative feedback, back off immediately and suggest making an appointment to talk again the following week. In other words, you should take off the pressure by being the one to withdraw first.

Often each partner in a couple is already sold, but they need time to talk over their decision in private. Make an excuse to leave the room for a few minutes. During this time ask your assistant to drop in on the couple and express her eagerness to work with them. However, make sure this tactic isn't obvious.

When you return, sit down and ask if there are any questions they would still like answered. If you have done your job well, their response should be "no". Then simply slide any necessary paperwork over to them with the words "Good. Let's get started just by moving this one account." As soon as they have signed, you have easily added a new client. You can be fairly sure you will continue to gain the rest of their assets.

You still want to ensure that they don't change their minds the next day. Take them on a tour of your office and introduce them to the rest of your staff. Make them feel they are part of your professional family. You may wish to give them your cell phone number in case they need to reach you after hours. You will find that most clients will not abuse that privilege. In short, do everything that their prior advisor didn't do. Finally, be sure to set up a meeting to take place as soon as the transfers are done. Your prospects have now become your clients.

# Conclusion

We hope reading <u>Marketing for Millions</u> has spurred some ideas and gotten your creative juices flowing – perhaps you even learned a few things along the way.

Now it's time to get down to business and start marketing.

While every financial advisor is unique, there is one common characteristic that all top producers share: *they have a system and they run it like a marketing machine.* Every time they give a seminar or send out a direct mail piece, they know through experience how many prospects they are going to generate and how many of those will eventually become clients. Once you reduce marketing to a predictable science like this, it virtually eliminates the risk. That is essentially what we've done for you in this book. The techniques are proven to work, you just need to make them your own and put them into effect.

You have a number of options available to you. But you also have to take an honest look at yourself. Are you seminar marketer? Would direct mail be a better fit for your market? Of course, your budget is also a major consideration. You have to decide how to invest your marketing dollars to minimize your risk and maximize your opportunity for success.

You have a lot of important decisions to make. Just as your clients rely on your financial expertise when making crucial investment choices, we hope you will look to the professionals at Acquire Direct Marketing as your trusted advisors when it comes to marketing your practice.

A consultation with one of our experienced financial marketing specialists will help you:

- Analyze the demographics of your target market
- Determine the budget necessary to implement your desired program
- Decide the best marketing approach for your practice
- Estimate the return on investment for your chosen direction

We have helped hundreds of advisors take their practice to the next level. We can do the same for you. If you think about it, our professions are really very similar. We both use our experience and knowledge to help others achieve financial success.

Give us a call.

Acquire Direct Marketing
800-771-9898
info@acquiredm.com

# Appendices

- Selecting A Venue Scorecard
- Attendee Tracking by Buying Units
- Cost Benefit Chart
- Seminar Checklist & Schedule
- Seminar Equipment Checklist
- Seminar Check-In Sheet
- "Seminar Confirmation" Letter
- Optional "Thank You for Attending" Letter
- "Seminar Welcome" Letter
- Seminar Appointment Card & Evaluation
- "Unable to Reach for First Appointment" Letter
- "Unable to Schedule an Appointment At This Time" Letter
- "First Appointment Confirmation" Letter
- "Second Appointment Confirmation" Letter
- "New Client" Letter
- "Refusal to Become a Client" Letter
- Financial Planning Guide *(Confidential)*
- Optional Risk Assessment Profile

# Selecting A Venue Scorecard

Selecting the right seminar venue is crucial. Use this checklist to score any restaurants, hotel meeting rooms or other venues you my be considering.

| SCORECARD FOR SEMINAR VENUES | YES | NO |
|---|---|---|
| 1. Is it accessible within twenty minutes driving time? | | |
| 2. Would your prospects consider it a treat to go there? | | |
| 3. Is there close, adequate free parking, or will the venue "comp" valet parking? | | |
| 4. How many will the room truly seat comfortably? Don't trust restaurant and hotel estimates without verifying with a walk-through | | |
| 5. Can the room be set up with round tables which are best for financial seminars? | | |
| 6. Do they have both medium and large round tables as well as six-foot rectangular tables for check-in staff and a small square table for your projector? | | |
| 7. Will they skirt the rectangular and square tables so that your gear and supply boxes can be hidden underneath? | | |
| 8. Are there adequate operational electrical wall outlets? | | |
| 9. Do they have a good internal dedicated sound system for your room? If not, will they provide one? | | |
| 10. Is there a pleasant place for smokers to take a break? | | |
| 11. Is there a back door to the meeting room with parking nearby so you can transport gear in and out without disturbing diners in the main restaurant? | | |
| 12. Will they set the room up completely one and a half hours in advance? (Some venues will delay setup as long as possible, leaving your prospects out in the cold while staff rolls in seating and tables.) | | |
| 13. Is there a waiting area with seating for early arrivals? | | |
| 14. Is there an adequate area for your sign in table? | | |
| 15. Is the room well kept, or is it a repository for storage or clutter? Many restaurants use meeting rooms to store extra tables, chairs and other paraphernalia. Clutter of this sort must be removed by the venue. | | |
| 16. Is there enough room for you, your projector and the screen? Make sure the screen can be easily seen by all attendees. Some meeting rooms are obstructed by pillars. Some are oddly shaped and will seat attendees in positions that make it impossible for guests to see the screen adequately | | |
| 17. Will the facility provide podiums, screens, and sound systems at little or no charge? | | |
| 18. Can you store bulky items at the facility in a secure location between seminars? (If you provide your own screen you will find it awkward to transport in all but the largest vehicles.) | | |
| 19. How often does the restaurant or hotel staff clean the restrooms and hallways? | | |
| 20. Will they provide a choice of entrees? If several entrees are available for your seminar, consider offering your guests a choice if they respond to the invitation promptly. | | |
| 21. Can you give the dining room a final meal count only twenty-four hours in advance? (Some attendees confirm or cancel the day before the event. You may be forced to order extra meals without knowing how many guests will attend if your venue demands a final meal count days in advance.) | | |
| 22. Will you be charged for no shows? | | |
| 23. Can the venue provide extra meals on one hour's notice in case of a last minute rush? (If you speak for an hour, that should be enough time for most restaurants to prepare extra meals.) | | |
| 24. Will the hotel or restaurant provide decorative table centerpieces and break table décor? | | |
| 25. Will the facility throw in extras such as a wide beverage selection? (Some offer only coffee, tea and water. Some charge exorbitant prices for mini bottles of soda pop.) | | |

# Selecting A Venue Scorecard - Continued

| SCORECARD FOR SEMINAR VENUES | YES | NO |
|---|---|---|
| 26. Will the dining room provide snacks at a reasonable cost? (It is helpful to provide your guests with a small protein-rich snack to make sure they are not thinking about a grumbling stomach instead of listening to you.) | | |
| 27. Will they give you at least one server for every twenty-four guests? | | |
| 28. Will you have to spend a lot on directional signage? (Many hotels require guests to navigate very complex routes to find meeting rooms. If the hotel does not offer signage or staff to direct guests as they arrive, you will need to make signs to guide the guests to your seminar. Clearly we prefer hotels and restaurants to assume this responsibility.) | | |
| 29. Is there a room fee in addition to the meal charge? | | |
| 30. What is the facility's minimum guarantee requirement? (Some hotels will require you to guarantee payment for a full dining or meeting room well in advance of your event. Don't sign a guarantee unless you are sure you will get value for your money.) | | |
| 31. Will the hotel or restaurant give you discounts for a long contract? (It is good if they will, but don't sign a long contract until you know how well the venue attracts clients.) | | |
| 32. Is the room completely soundproof? (Many hotels separate meeting rooms with supposedly soundproof barriers. These rarely work perfectly if there is a meeting being held in the next room at the same time as yours. We prefer separate rooms for seminars, but if you must agree to soundproof moveable walls, ask the hotel or restaurant to guarantee that your audience will not be distracted during your all-important speech.) | | |
| 33. Are the temperature controls working perfectly? (Often seniors at a seminar will complain that a meeting room is too cold.) Is there a staff member you can always contact easily to adjust room temperature? We suggest that you keep a few inexpensive sweaters among your seminar supplies for attendees who will complain of the cold no matter what the room temperature. | | |
| 34. Room lighting is important. Is there a place you can stand that will project a flattering light on you while leaving the screen area dark? (Too often we have seen presenters giving their talk in a pool of darkness because lights have been dimmed for the projector. If the venue cannot adjust the room light so you have a well-lit area to speak from, consider bringing some simple lights. It is essential that the audience see your face during the entire seminar.) | | |
| 35. Are the outside views too distracting? (Sometimes restaurants are unable to close windows or openings to other parts of the facility. Excessive outside activity can distract audience attention. Excessive outside light can make your screen hard to see. Make sure you are satisfied that curtains and room dividers are adequate to prevent visual distractions.) | | |
| 36. Will kitchen and wait staff respect your privacy? (Too often we have seen seminars disrupted by thoughtless staff. Sometimes kitchens adjoin the meeting room and your speech may be interrupted by crashing dishes, shouted orders, laughter and loud conversation. In rare cases wait staff will walk through meeting rooms to serve other areas. This must not be allowed.) | | |
| 37. Obtain a sample contract and a copy of your table layout for your files. Bring these documents to every event in case of disputes. | | |
| 38. Is the room wheelchair accessible? (The law requires handicapped access, but not all facilities provide access that will be acceptable to an audience that may include many seniors arriving at once.) | | |
| 39. Have you visited the location personally? (Not just your staff.) | | |
| **Score Each Venue with a Total of Positives and Negatives** | | |

# Attendee Tracking by Buying Units

Seminar Date, Location and Presentation Type _____

| Last Name & First Names | Address | City | Zip | Phone | Attended Seminar? | Referrals or Guests? | Booked Appointment at Seminar or by phone? | Confirmation Calls & Letters | First Appointment | Result | Second Appointment | Result | Notes for Future Action? | First Quarter Income | First Year Income | Second Year Income |
|---|---|---|---|---|---|---|---|---|---|---|---|---|---|---|---|---|
| 1 | | | | | | | | | | | | | | | | |
| 2 | | | | | | | | | | | | | | | | |
| 3 | | | | | | | | | | | | | | | | |
| 4 | | | | | | | | | | | | | | | | |
| 5 | | | | | | | | | | | | | | | | |

3/3/2007

# Cost Benefit Chart

## Seminar Tracking Data

|  | Group 1 | Group 2 | Group 3 | Group 4 |
|---|---|---|---|---|
| Seminar Date or Group of Dates |  |  |  |  |
| Size of Mailing |  |  |  |  |
| Invitation Used |  |  |  |  |
| Zip Codes Mailed to |  |  |  |  |
| Seminar Location & Type |  |  |  |  |
| Number of Confirmations |  |  |  |  |
| Number Of Attendees (Buying Units) |  |  |  |  |
| Number Asking For Appts at Seminar |  |  |  |  |
| Number Reached by Phone |  |  |  |  |
| Attendees Booking Appointments |  |  |  |  |
| Number of "Call me later" |  |  |  |  |
| Reason |  |  |  |  |
| Number saying "No" |  |  |  |  |
| Reason |  |  |  |  |
| Total First Appointments Held |  |  |  |  |
| Number Booking 2nd App:s |  |  |  |  |
| Total Second Appointments Held |  |  |  |  |
| Total Closings For This Seminar |  |  |  |  |
| Notes: |  |  |  |  |

## Cost Tracking Data

|  | Group 1 | Group 2 | Group 3 | Group 4 |
|---|---|---|---|---|
| Invitations |  |  |  |  |
| Restaurant |  |  |  |  |
| Audio Visual |  |  |  |  |
| Staff |  |  |  |  |
| Miscellaneous |  |  |  |  |
| **Total Costs For This Seminar Group** |  |  |  |  |
| Calculate Cost Per Attendee (BU) |  |  |  |  |
| Business Written 3 Months |  |  |  |  |
| Business Written 1 Year |  |  |  |  |

3/3/2007

# Seminar Checklist & Schedule

- [ ] CHECK PARKING LOT FOR ADEQUATE PARKING SPACES
- [ ] CHECK EXTERIOR OF BUILDING TO ENSURE CLEANLINESS
- [ ] MAKE SURE CORRIDORS TO SEMINAR ARE CLEAN
- [ ] CHECK LIGHTING AND ELECTRICAL SOCKETS
- [ ] MAKE SURE VENUE HAS SET UP RISER IF NEEDED
- [ ] MAKE SURE STOOL AND/OR PODIUM IN PLACE
- [ ] SET UP PROJECTION TABLE
- [ ] SET UP SCREEN
- [ ] MAKE SURE 8 FOOT BREAK TABLE IS SET UP
- [ ] MAKE SURE TABLES ARE IN PROPER CONFIGURATION
- [ ] PLACE 4 TO 6 CHAIRS IN BACK OF ROOM FOR LATE ARRIVALS
- [ ] SET UP PODIUM WITH PAPERS, TENSOR LIGHT, CLOCK, WATER
- [ ] SET UP SOUND SYSTEM
- [ ] TEST SOUND SYSTEM WHEN SPEAKER ARRIVES SPECIFICALLY FOR SPEAKERS VOICE
- [ ] TAPE DOWN CORDS AND HIDE EXCESS CORDS
- [ ] TEST SIGHT LINES SITTING IN VARIOUS CHAIRS AROUND THE ROOM
- [ ] GET STAFF TO SET UP (8 FOOT) SIGN-IN TABLE WITH 2 CHAIRS AND WASTEBASKET

## ONE HOUR AND FIFTEEN MINUTES BEFORE START OF EVENT

- [ ] MAKE SURE ALL TABLES (BREAK, PROJECTOR AND SIGN IN) HAVE LINEN AND ARE SKIRTED. ALSO ANY FILLER TABLES BEHIND SCREEN.
- [ ] ALL SIGNAGE SHOULD BE PUT IN PLACE
- [ ] MAKE SURE ALL DINNER TABLES ARE SET WITH SILVERWARE ROLLUPS, WATER GLASSES & CENTERPIECES
- [ ] WASTEBASKET BENEATH BREAK TABLE
- [ ] EXTRA SUPPLIES BENEATH BREAK TABLE:
    - CREAM
    - LEMON WEDGES
    - SUGAR & DIET SWEETENER
    - NAPKINS
    - SPOONS
    - EXTRA PLATES, CUPS, SPOONS
    - COOKIE TRAYS - PASS OUT IMMEDIATELY AT BREAK

# Seminar Checklist & Schedule  - Continued

**ONE HOUR BEFORE EVENT**

☐ ENSURE THAT SIGN-IN TABLE IS FULLY SET UP WITH CENTERPIECE, PACKETS, NAME TAGS, PENS AND A WASTEBASKET BELOW THE TABLE

**45 MINUTES BEFORE EVENT**

☐ HAVE STAFF DO FINAL VACUUM AND REMOVE ANY CLUTTER

☐ DO FINAL CHECK OF ENTRANCE AND RESTROOMS TO MAKE SURE THEY ARE CLEAN

☐ RAISE ROOM TEMPERATURE

☐ TURN ON SOFT MUSIC

☐ HAVE STAFF FILL WATER GLASSES ON DINING TABLES

☐ BREAK TABLE SHOULD BE READY WITH THE FOLLOWING:
  ICE
  COFFEE (REGULAR & DECAF)
  HOT TEA (REGULAR & DECAF)
  ICED TEA
  ONE SPECIAL BEVERAGE (SODA, LEMONADE, ETC.)
  CUT LEMON WEDGES
  SUGAR & ARTIFICIAL SWEETENER
  CUPS BESIDE HOT TEA AND COFFEE
  GLASSES BESIDE ICE AND SODA
  CREAM BESIDE COFFEE

**ONE HALF HOUR BEFORE EVENT**

☐ OPEN DOORS AND BEGIN SIGN IN

**EXACT START TIME OF EVENT**

☐ IF PEOPLE ARE MISSING GIVE HOUSEKEEPING SPEECH

(ANNOUNCE THAT EVENT WILL START IN FIVE MINUTES. WAITING ON LATE ARRIVALS. INQUIRE ABOUT COMFORT OF TEMPERATURE)

**FIVE MINUTES AFTER EVENT WAS DUE TO START**

☐ DIM LIGHTS

☐ TURN DOWN MUSIC

☐ GIVE INTRODUCTION

**RIGHT BEFORE BREAK**

☐ CHECK RESTROOMS TO MAKE SURE THEY ARE CLEAN

☐ BRING OUT TRAYS OF COOKIES

# Seminar Equipment Checklist

## Equipment

☐ COMPUTER

☐ PROJECTOR

☐ TABLE FOR PROJECTOR

☐ SPARE PROJECTOR BULB

☐ TWO POWER STRIPS

☐ THREE EXTENSION CORDS

☐ SOUND SYSTEM (Fender Passport)

☐ WIRLESS MIC, LAVALIER

☐ HAND MIC FOR INTRO

☐ R.F. MOUSE

☐ WHITEBOARD, MARKERS, ERASERS

☐ SCISSORS

☐ GAFFER TAPE

☐ GOO GONE

☐ SPEAKER STANDS

☐ CLOCK FOR PODIUM

☐ SPEAKER'S WATER PITCHER

☐ HANDOUTS

☐ NOTEPADS & EXTRA PENS

☐ TENSOR LIGHT FOR PODIUM

☐ COPY OF PRESENTATION IN BINDER

☐ STAND FOR WHITEBOARD OR FLIPCHART

## Signage

☐ DIRECTIONS AT ENTRANCE

## Provided By Venue?

☐ RISER IF NEEDED

☐ STOOL

☐ FREESTANDING PODIUM

☐ SCREEN

☐ MUSIC, IF NEEDED

☐ SUPPORT FOR SIGNAGE

## Miscellaneous (For Seminars)

☐ ATTENDEE LIST (2 COPIES)

☐ ID TAGS FOR STAFF

☐ NAME TAGS

☐ SWEATERS FOR SENIORS

☐ SIGNAGE FOR PODIUM

☐ BREAK TABLE SETUP

☐ RESERVED TABLE SIGNS

☐ SIGN-IN TABLE SIGNAGE

☐ DECORATIONS

☐ OUTSIDE PROTEIN-BASED SNACKS

☐ **Don't Forget Batteries For Everything!**

☐ OTHER: _____

_____

# Seminar Check-In Sheet

| Last Name | First Names | Address | City | Zip | Phone | Attended Seminar? | Referrals or Guests? | Booked Appointme't at Seminar or by phone? | Notes |
|---|---|---|---|---|---|---|---|---|---|
| | | | | | | | | | |
| | | | | | | | | | |
| | | | | | | | | | |
| | | | | | | | | | |
| | | | | | | | | | |
| | | | | | | | | | |
| | | | | | | | | | |
| | | | | | | | | | |
| | | | | | | | | | |
| | | | | | | | | | |

3/3/2007

# "Seminar Confirmation" Letter

Mr. and Mrs. John Doe
xxxxxxxxxxxxxxxxxx
xxxxxxxxxxxxxxxxxx

Dear Mr. and Mrs. Doe: *(mail merge)*

This letter is just to let you know that we have reserved seats for you for our upcoming seminar on  (Seminar Topic) . The date and time of the seminar are _____. We have also reserved seats for your guests, _____ and _____. We will confirm with them separately.

Please remember to bring the tickets that were enclosed in the invitation and remember that we always start promptly. Dinner will be served after the presentation.

You will find a map in this envelope and instructions on how to use the complimentary parking. Please note that we have also taken care of the parking gratuity.

If for any reason you are unable to attend, please let us know as soon as possible because there is a waiting list for this event.

We look forward to meeting you in person at the seminar. If you have any questions please do not hesitate to call us at _____.

With best regards,

Seminar Coordinator

# Optional "Thank You for Attending" Letter

(to be sent out on the Morning of the Seminar)

Mr. and Mrs. John Doe
xxxxxxxxxxxxxxxxxx
xxxxxxxxxxxxxxxxxx


Dear Mr. and Mrs. Doe: *(mail merge)*

We just want to say thank you for joining us for our seminar
on _____ at the _____.
We sincerely hope you found the evening both enjoyable and
constructive. Our seminars are designed to demonstrate our
commitment to the financial education of our community.

If we can provide you with additional information, please
feel free to contact us so we can set up an appointment which
involves no obligation. We set aside several days after each
seminar in order to answer any questions the attendees might
have.

We look forward to helping you in any way we can. Again,
thanks for coming.

Sincerely,


Advisor

## "Seminar Welcome" Letter

Dear Mr. and Mrs. Doe: *(mail merge)*

Welcome to our newly updated financial seminar on  (Seminar Topic) .

We sincerely hope you find tonight's presentation stimulating and thought provoking. We encourage you to take notes on the paper provided. We also suggest that you make a check mark in the box beside any subject that interests you on the evaluation and appointment card enclosed in this packet.

If this educational seminar raises any questions or concerns about your financial situation, we will be happy to offer you a complimentary "get acquainted" appointment to provide more information. This appointment will not include any sales presentation.

Our first concern tonight is that you enjoy your evening. We hope the dinner will be to your liking and that you learn some valuable new insights from our presentation. Feel free to ask us questions afterwards or make an appointment for a no obligation consultation. We wish you a secure and prosperous retirement.

Once again, thank you. We are glad you came.

Yours truly,

Advisor

# Seminar Appointment Card & Evaluation

Name of Guest_____ Phone Number_____

I WOULD PREFER TO TAKE ADVANTAGE OF MY COMPLIMENTARY APPOINTMENT
ON _____ AT_____.

(CIRCLE PREFERENCES)

THE BEST DAY TO REACH ME BY TELEPHONE IS:

MONDAY     TUESDAY     WEDNESDAY     THURSDAY     FRIDAY

I PREFER TO BE CALLED IN THE:

MORNING           AFTERNOON           EVENING

The topics discussed during the presentation that are of interest to me were:

☐ xxxxxxxx     ☐ xxxxxxxx     ☐ xxxxxxxx     ☐ xxxxxxxx

☐ xxxxxxxx     ☐ xxxxxxxx     ☐ xxxxxxxx     ☐ xxxxxxxx

Other topics of interest_____.

How would you describe the content of the seminar and the quality of the
speaker?

_____

_____.

Do you have any friends you would like us to contact who might also benefit
from this presentation?_____.

Thank you for completing this form, Dinner will be served as soon as all
forms are collected.

# "Unable to Reach for First Appointment" Letter

Mr. and Mrs. John Doe
xxxxxxxxxxxxxxxxxx
xxxxxxxxxxxxxxxxxx


Dear Mr. and Mrs. Doe:

Our office has tried to contact you several times since you attended our financial seminar. As I mentioned at the seminar, we try to help people maximize their returns and lower their taxes, but it is difficult to do anything without a first meeting. That first appointment is simply an opportunity to meet each other, and it gives you something to think over.

During our visit I may be able to make some suggestions to help your financial situation. On the other hand, the meeting may serve as a time to verify that everything seems fine as it is. In either case, it should be time well spent. We have served many happy clients over the years, and it is our wish to be of service to you.

I would greatly appreciate it if you could give me a courtesy call to let me know your thoughts.

Sincerely yours,

Advisor

# "Unable to Schedule an Appointment at This Time" Letter

Mr. and Mrs. John Doe
xxxxxxxxxxxxxxxxxxx
xxxxxxxxxxxxxxxxxx


Dear Mr. and Mrs. Doe:

It was a pleasure speaking with you today. I am glad to hear you enjoyed the dinner. I hope I was able to address some of your concerns during the course of the seminar.

I understand that you are unable to commit to an appointment until _(excuse)_. I have marked my calendar to contact you in approximately one month. Remember there is absolutely no charge for this visit. We will discuss your needs and concerns at that time. It's painless, it's free and always worth your while.

Over the years we have had the privilege of helping many individuals face many challenging situations. I hope you will become one of our satisfied clients. We'll look forward to talking with you again next month.

Sincerely yours,

Advisor

# "First Appointment Confirmation" Letter

Mr. and Mrs. John Doe
xxxxxxxxxxxxxxxxxxx
xxxxxxxxxxxxxxxxxx


Dear Mr. and Mrs. Doe:

We are so glad you have decided to take advantage of our complimentary appointment. You can expect the meeting to take between forty-five minutes and an hour. We promise it will be well worth your time.

In order to give you the best analysis of your current financial situation, we request you bring along the following papers:

        1.xxxxxxxxxxxxxxxx
        2.xxxxxxxxxxxxxxxx
        3.xxxxxxxxxxxxxxxx
        4.xxxxxxxxxxxxxxxx

We view this appointment as a way to get to know each other better. There will be no discussion of sales or products. We look forward to seeing you on _____ at_____. Please let us know right away if you are unable to keep this time so we can make other arrangements.

You will find a map to the location of our office enclosed. There is reserved parking for our clients at _____.

We look forward to seeing you on _____.

With warmest regards,

Advisor

# "Second Appointment Confirmation" Letter

Mr. and Mrs. John Doe
xxxxxxxxxxxxxxxxxxx
xxxxxxxxxxxxxxxxxxx

Dear Mr. and Mrs. Doe:

It was both a pleasure and a privilege to meet with you today. I hope you found the experience as enjoyable and constructive as I did. It is my understanding that you do have concerns about your future, particularly in the areas of _____ and _____. With your permission I would like to do some additional research in order to give you the best solutions possible.

If your goals are different from those stated above, feel free to give me a call. After all, it is my main desire to provide you with the financial security you seek while _____. This will be the primary agenda for our appointment.

As you may remember, I requested that you bring in extra materials that I can use during the course of my analysis. If there is any way I might receive them prior to our next meeting, that would be most helpful.

I shall anticipate seeing you on _____ at_____.

Best regards,

Advisor

# "New Client" Letter

Mr. and Mrs. John Doe
xxxxxxxxxxxxxxxxxx
xxxxxxxxxxxxxxxxxx

Dear Mr. and Mrs. Doe:

Welcome and thank you! We are both pleased and flattered that you have selected our firm to work with you in achieving your goal of establishing a prosperous financial future. We shall endeavor to make you one of our highly satisfied clients.

As soon as the proper paperwork has been transferred over, you will receive a call from us to set up your next appointment. At that time we will begin to think about implementing those strategies we discussed at our prior meetings. Of course, while we wish to take action on anything that requires our immediate attention, we also want to proceed with other longer term goals in a deliberate and measured manner.

If you have any concerns or questions before our next meeting, we would be happy to help.

Once again, thank you for becoming part of our financial family.

Very truly yours,

Advisor

# "Refusal to Become a Client" Letter

Mr. and Mrs. John Doe
xxxxxxxxxxxxxxxxxx
xxxxxxxxxxxxxxxxxx

Dear Mr. and Mrs. Doe:

Thank you for taking the time to consider letting me serve you. I sincerely regret that your immediate plans do not include developing a relationship at this time.

We constantly stay informed of new developments and strategies for higher returns and lower taxes, so please don't hesitate to contact me if you should change your mind.

I am enclosing a few of my business cards, and I thank you in advance for placing them in the hands of any of your friends or acquaintances whom I might be able to serve. Much of my business is built on referrals and word of mouth.

Thanks again,

Advisor

# Financial Planning Guide

## (Confidential)

Name _____ DOB _____

Spouse's Name _____ DOB _____

Address _____

Phone (Home) _____ Phone (Business) _____

Social Security # _____ Social Security # _____

| Children | Ages | State of Residence |
|---|---|---|
| _____ | _____ | _____ |
| _____ | _____ | _____ |
| _____ | _____ | _____ |
| _____ | _____ | _____ |
| _____ | _____ | _____ |

| Grandchildren | Ages | State of Residence |
|---|---|---|
| _____ | _____ | _____ |
| _____ | _____ | _____ |
| _____ | _____ | _____ |
| _____ | _____ | _____ |

## Personal Questions

| | Yes | No |
|---|---|---|
| Are you happy with your current financial advisor? | | |
| Do you have an accountant? | | |
| Do you have an attorney? | | |
| Are your estate documents in order? | | |
| Do you have Long Term Care protection? | | |
| Do you expect an inheritance? | | |
| Are you facing any unusual expense? | | |
| Do you do your own investing? | | |
| Do you have any investments you do not wish to change? | | |
| Do you have any investments you do wish to change? | | |
| Are you comfortable with risk? | | |

## Sources of Monthly Income

| SOCIAL SECURITY | |
|---|---|
| Husband | $ |
| Wife | $ |
| **PENSION** | |
| Husband | $ |
| Wife | $ |
| **WAGES** | |
| Husband | $ |
| Wife | $ |
| **REAL ESTATE** | $ |
| **DIVIDENDS** | $ |
| **INTEREST** | $ |
| OTHER | $ |
| OTHER | $ |
| **TOTAL** | $ |

**How Much Did You Pay in Taxes Last Year?**

_____

**Estimated Monthly Expenditure**

_____

**What is the most important financial issue I can help you solve?** _____

_____

# Financial Planning Guide - Continued

*(Confidential)*

| Real Estate | |
|---|---|
| Home Value | $ |
| Mortgage | $ |
| **Equity** | $ |
| Other Real Estate Equity | $ |
| **Total Real Estate Equity** | $ |

| Retirement Accounts | | |
|---|---|---|
| **Custodian** | **Type** | **Amount** |
| | | $ |
| | | $ |
| | | $ |
| | | $ |

| Life Insurance | | | | | | |
|---|---|---|---|---|---|---|
| Company | Type | Face Amount | Cash Value | Premium | Insured | Beneficiary |
| | | | | | | |
| | | | | | | |
| | | | | | | |

| Amounts in Banks, Savings & Loans, Credit Unions (Non IRA) | | |
|---|---|---|
| Institution | Type of Account | Balance |
| | | |
| | | |
| | | |

| CDs | | | |
|---|---|---|---|
| Issuing Institution | Rate of Return | Amount Invested | Maturity Date |
| | | | |
| | | | |

| Individual Stocks & Bonds | | | | | | |
|---|---|---|---|---|---|---|
| Name of Investment | # of shares | Purchase Date | Original Investment | Market Value | Ownership | Custodian |
| | | | | | | |
| | | | | | | |
| | | | | | | |
| | | | | | | |
| | | | | | | |
| | | | | | | |

| Mutual Funds & Limited or General Partnerships | | | | | | |
|---|---|---|---|---|---|---|
| Name & Type of Investment | # of shares | Purchase Date | Original Investment | Market Value | Ownership | Custodian |
| | | | | | | |
| | | | | | | |
| | | | | | | |
| | | | | | | |
| | | | | | | |

| Annuities | | | | | | |
|---|---|---|---|---|---|---|
| Company | Type | Purchase Date | Investment | Current Value | Interest Rate | Owner |
| | | | | | | |
| | | | | | | |
| | | | | | | |

| Other | | | | | |
|---|---|---|---|---|---|
| Type | Purchase Date | Investment | Current Value | Interest Rate? Or Return | Owner |
| | | | | | |
| | | | | | |
| | | | | | |

# Financial Planning Guide - Continued

*(Confidential)*

## 1. Personal Questions

|  | Yes | No |
|---|---|---|
| 1. Do you have a Financial Advisor? (No stockbrokers, please) If yes, who? _____ | ❏ | ❏ |
| 2. Do you have a living trust? | ❏ | ❏ |
| 3. Do you have a will? | ❏ | ❏ |
| 4. Do you have income from real estate? | ❏ | ❏ |
| 5. Do you have an attorney? | ❏ | ❏ |
| 6. Do you have an accountant? | ❏ | ❏ |
| 7. Do you expect to care for a child/parent? | ❏ | ❏ |
| 8. Do you expect an inheritance? | ❏ | ❏ |
| 9. Any problems with previous stockbrokers? | ❏ | ❏ |
| 10. Do you have long term care protection? | ❏ | ❏ |

## 2. Financial Planning Objectives

Rank the following according to your level of concern.
*(Please circle the most appropriate number)*

| | Not Concerned | Very Concerned |
|---|---|---|
| Planning for children or Grandchildren | 1 2 3 4 5 6 7 8 9 10 | |
| Reducing Current Income Taxes | 1 2 3 4 5 6 7 8 9 10 | |
| Increasing Current Income | 1 2 3 4 5 6 7 8 9 10 | |
| Estate Planning | 1 2 3 4 5 6 7 8 9 10 | |
| Desire for Professional Management | 1 2 3 4 5 6 7 8 9 10 | |
| Maximum Growth | 1 2 3 4 5 6 7 8 9 10 | |
| Combined Growth/Income | 1 2 3 4 5 6 7 8 9 10 | |

## 3. Real Estate

| | |
|---|---|
| Estimated Value of Home | $ _____ |
| Remaining Mortgage | $ _____ |
| Equity in Home (market value less mortgage) | $ _____ |
| Other Real Estate | $ _____ |
| Remaining Mortgage | $ _____ |
| Total Value of Real Estate | $ _____ |

## 4. Sources of Monthly Retirement Income

| SOCIAL SECURITY | |
|---|---|
| You | $ _____ |
| Spouse | $ _____ |
| PENSION | |
| You | $ _____ |
| Spouse | $ _____ |

## 5. Bank and Credit Union Inventory

(Checking, Savings, Money Market Accounts)

| | Name of Institution | Average Balance |
|---|---|---|
| 1. | _____ | _____ |
| 2. | _____ | _____ |
| 3. | _____ | _____ |
| 4. | _____ | _____ |
| 5. | _____ | _____ |

*(Confidential)*

## 6. Collectibles/Collections *(coins, stamps, etc.)*

| Item | Estimated Value |
|---|---|
| _____ | $ _____ |
| _____ | $ _____ |
| _____ | $ _____ |
| _____ | $ _____ |

## 7. Current Stockbrokers

(Please CHECK any brokerage firms
  you have an account with)

❑ Merrill Lynch          ❑ Smith Barney
❑ A.G. Edwards           ❑ Prudential
❑ Raymond James          ❑ Paine Webber
❑ Charles Schwab         ❑ Other_____
❑ Other _____      ❑ Other_____
❑ Other _____      ❑ Other_____

## 8. Individual Stocks & Bonds - Please include EE Bonds

(Do not include mutual funds or IRA's here)    (Please bring all statements)

| Number of Shares | Name of Company | Original Investment | Market Value | Ownership | Date Acquired |
|---|---|---|---|---|---|
| _____ | _____ | $ _____ | $ _____ | _____ | _____ |
| _____ | _____ | $ _____ | $ _____ | _____ | _____ |
| _____ | _____ | $ _____ | $ _____ | _____ | _____ |
| _____ | _____ | $ _____ | $ _____ | _____ | _____ |
| _____ | _____ | $ _____ | $ _____ | _____ | _____ |
| _____ | _____ | $ _____ | $ _____ | _____ | _____ |

## 9. Mutual Funds/Limited Partnerships

| Number of Shares | Name of Company | Original Investment | Market Value | Ownership | Date Acquired |
|---|---|---|---|---|---|
| _____ | _____ | $ _____ | $ _____ | _____ | _____ |
| _____ | _____ | $ _____ | $ _____ | _____ | _____ |
| _____ | _____ | $ _____ | $ _____ | _____ | _____ |
| _____ | _____ | $ _____ | $ _____ | _____ | _____ |
| _____ | _____ | $ _____ | $ _____ | _____ | _____ |
| _____ | _____ | $ _____ | $ _____ | _____ | _____ |

## 10. CD's

| Name of Bank | Rate of Return | Amt. Invested | Maturity Date |
|---|---|---|---|
| _____ | _____ | _____ | _____ |
| _____ | _____ | _____ | _____ |
| _____ | _____ | _____ | _____ |
| _____ | _____ | _____ | _____ |

## 11. IRA & Other Retirement Account Information
(Please bring in latest reports/statements)

| | Name Where Account Is (Bank, Broker, Employer) | Type (401k, IRA, 403b, TSA) | Approximate Value |
|---|---|---|---|
| 1. | _____ | _____ | _____ |
| 2. | _____ | _____ | _____ |
| 3. | _____ | _____ | _____ |
| 4. | _____ | _____ | _____ |

## 12. Present Life Insurance

| Company | Type | Face Amount | Cash Value | Annual Premium | Who Is Insured | Who Is Beneficiary |
|---|---|---|---|---|---|---|
| _____ | _____ | _____ | _____ | _____ | _____ | _____ |
| _____ | _____ | _____ | _____ | _____ | _____ | _____ |
| _____ | _____ | _____ | _____ | _____ | _____ | _____ |
| _____ | _____ | _____ | _____ | _____ | _____ | _____ |

## 13. Annuities

| Company | Original Investment | Date Purchased |
|---|---|---|
| _____ | _____ | _____ |
| _____ | _____ | _____ |
| _____ | _____ | _____ |
| _____ | _____ | _____ |

## Other Notes:

_____

_____

_____

_____

# Optional Risk Assessment Profile

1. What is or has been the greatest total value of your investable assets over the last five years?

   _____

2. What is or has been the lowest total value of your investable assets over the last five years?

   _____

3. To what do you attribute any loss of your assets?   _____

   _____

4. What percentage of loss of assets would be unacceptable to you? _____

5. What is the rate of return exclusive of fees you are expecting on your assets over the next

   One Year Period? _____     Three Year Period? _____     Five Year Period? _____

6. Check which word or words describe your primary goal.
   ❑ Growth     ❑ Rapid Growth     ❑ Income     ❑ Tax Avoidance     ❑ Estate Planning

7. Are both parties involved in agreement over the chief objective of the account?

   _____

8. Would both parties be willing to sign a risk tolerance agreement? _____

9. How much input would you like to have regarding the employment of financial strategies and

   investment decisions?_____

Notes: